1007/49'23

f.7

THE
ARCHITECT
OF THE NEW
BJP

ADVANCE PRAISE FOR THE BOOK

'Repeated election victories require not just a charismatic leader but also the creation of organizations and institutions that last. In this engaging book, Ajay Singh offers the reader an unusual peek into Narendra Modi the builder, beginning with the story of his impeccable organization of relief work following the 1979 Machchhu River dam tragedy in Gujarat all the way down to his transformation of India's economy and polity today'—Arvind Panagariya, professor, Columbia University, and author of *India Unlimited*

'The world has witnessed the meteoric rise of Narendra Modi, from a *chaiwallah* to India's *pradhan mantri*! But how? Ajay Singh provides a riveting, behind-the-scenes narrative of Modi's organizational skills, discipline against all odds, stern empathy, self-reflection and perseverance that scripted his success. Inspirational, informative and engaging'—S.P. Kothari, Gordon Y. Billard Professor of Accounting and Finance, MIT Sloan School of Management

'The electoral magic of Modi seems to be getting stronger every day. Of course, his charisma and personal appeal are unparalleled, but a secret of his success is his organizational genius that he used to reinvent the BJP into a political entity transcending geographical, demographic and economic barriers. Ajay Singh's book is the first credible attempt to analyse how Modi transformed a legacy organization to power his success and create the most successful political party since Independence'—Uday Shankar, former president, Walt Disney APAC, and former chairman, Star India

'There is a time in a leader's life before the figure is in full glare of the public eye. These years hold clues to more than we may admit. Ajay Singh gives us rare insights into the work and manner of India's prime minister. Perhaps more than others, this is a veteran reporter's angle'—Mahesh Rangarajan, environmental historian and political analyst

'An informative, evidence-based book which unfolds the story of the long political journey of Narendra Modi, from being a modest Sangh *pracharak* to becoming one of the most powerful prime ministers of India. What makes this book interesting is the author's close look at the organizational skills of Narendra Modi, which he demonstrated when he was a lesser-known politician. This book presents a detailed account of Modi's organizational skills, his courage to experiment and innovate, beyond traditional vote-bank politics, even when he had just made an entry in electoral politics from the Sangh Parivar'—Sanjay Kumar, professor, the Centre for the Study of Developing Societies (CSDS), Delhi

THE
ARCHITECT
OF THE NEW
BJP

HOW **NARENDRA MODI**
TRANSFORMED THE PARTY

Foreword by WALTER ANDERSEN

To,
Dear David

AJAY SINGH

With best wishes

Ajay

VINTAGE
An imprint of Penguin Random House

VINTAGE

USA | Canada | UK | Ireland | Australia
New Zealand | India | South Africa | China

Vintage is part of the Penguin Random House group of companies
whose addresses can be found at global.penguinrandomhouse.com

Published by Penguin Random House India Pvt. Ltd
4th Floor, Capital Tower 1, MG Road,
Gurugram 122 002, Haryana, India

Penguin
Random House
India

First published in Vintage by Penguin Random House India 2022

Copyright © Ajay Singh 2022
Foreword copyright © Walter Andersen 2022

All rights reserved

10 9 8 7 6 5 4 3

ISBN 9780670096961

Typeset in Adobe Caslon Pro by Manipal Technologies Limited, Manipal
Printed at Thomson Press India Ltd, New Delhi

www.penguin.co.in

MIX
Paper
FSC FSC® C010615

In memory of my mother

Contents

Foreword

Ajay Singh has written an important book that analyses Prime Minister Narendra Modi's impressive organizational skills used to build the Bharatiya Janata Party (BJP) as India's predominant political party and, in the process, advancing his own career path to the position of prime minister. The prime minister's shrewd political skills were again witnessed in the run-up to the recent assembly election. On 10 March 2022, the BJP was announced as the winner in four of the five states that had voted, with a spectacular victory in Uttar Pradesh, India's most populous state. The BJP's electoral performance in these states seems to affirm Ajay Singh's key propositions regarding Modi's ability to successfully use the party organization as the interface between the people and what they want on the one side and the government/bureaucracy on the other. Much of the book is an analysis of why Singh thinks this system is likely to survive even when Modi fades from the political scene.

A study of any organization requires a deep insight into its functioning, which is why many scholars analysing political parties either avoid this difficult task or provide only a cursory analysis. Singh is an exception; he knows many of the key figures that are the subject of the book and brings to his study the insights and contacts that he had gained as a journalist working on national political issues. Unlike so many studies of

Modi, this is not a book that relies almost exclusively on news reports and quotes that appear in the press. Nor does it have an agenda aimed primarily at condemning or praising.

One of the strengths of this book is his analysis of the factors contributing to Modi's organizational skills. Among the most important are (1) the focused self-discipline expected of every member of his poor, religiously inclined Gujarati family to work together systematically for its well-being, and (2) his participation from the age of eight in the daily meetings at the local Rashtriya Swayamsevak Sangh (RSS) unit with its focus on self-discipline and building a cohesive nation within a Hindu cultural context. The key elements of the RSS's operational style (which the RSS defines as 'character building') impressed Modi, and the RSS became for him a kind of surrogate family. As was noted in our book on the functioning of the RSS and its affiliates, *The Brotherhood in Saffron*, a major reason for its cohesiveness and influence was its decision-making system relying on organizing secretaries (referred to as the *sangathan* model) composed mostly of people who have demonstrated loyalty to the RSS and its ideology to ensure that specific goals are achieved within the organization's ideological parameters.* This was a system adopted by all the affiliated organizations of the RSS, including the BJP.

Ajay Singh notes throughout the book that this system appealed to Modi's own commitment to getting things done, which was almost certainly influenced by his family, especially his mother. Modi was also fortunate in 1982 to link up with the current home minister and his closest confidant and political adviser, Amit Shah, early in his political career. Coming from a successful business family in Mumbai and an RSS member, Shah

---

* For an extensive discussion of this decision-making system in the RSS, see Walter K. Andersen and Shridhar D. Damle, *The Brotherhood in Saffron*, Penguin, 2019.

was totally loyal to Modi, and he brought to the relationship the tough-minded pragmatism that leaders like Modi often rely on to make difficult campaign decisions and personnel choices, including cracking down on dissidents and opponents. The two proved successful in unifying a faction-ridden BJP in Gujarat and then at the national level. Shah also orchestrated the BJP's two successful national parliamentary campaigns (2014 and 2019). Through all this, he remained at Modi's side. He has a sufficiently close relationship with the prime minister to be frank with him.

Modi moved beyond the RSS's narrow sangathan model to mobilize voter support, though, as Singh points out, he retained it to the extent that he could staff the party organization by relying on full-time RSS workers and fill the party's organizational positions at senior levels. During his three terms as chief minister and working closely with Amit Shah in Gujarat, Modi constructed an electoral strategy that involved recruiting influential leaders in every village and city, whatever their past politics—a tactic long associated with the Congress party. But this recruitment tactic did not undermine the party's larger Hindu ideological orientation because the party's leadership at every level was largely drawn from the RSS. In addition, Modi supervised the establishment of voter groups in every voting booth to enhance personal involvement that builds commitment, a tactic that Shah and Modi may have learnt from the RSS, which has used personal involvement in its local units and in such activities as flood and earthquake relief, and, more recently, in responding to the social dislocations caused by the successive COVID outbreaks in India.

The electoral success of this strategy cemented Shah's links to Modi. It led to three successive victories for the BJP in the Gujarat assembly (2002, 2007 and 2012) and was carried over nationally to the successful BJP parliamentary campaigns in 2014 and 2019, with the party winning a majority on its own. These national victories altered several widely held perceptions of the BJP: it was not limited to the upper castes and urban areas, and to the so-called cow belt of north–central India, though it remains relatively weak in the south. It has spread into rural India and now has its own robust farm affiliate. Despite the party's electoral successes, there has been some pushback from RSS stalwarts in the party (and some within the RSS itself) over Modi's tactic of recruiting outsiders, fearing that the BJP would become more like the detested Congress. But the electoral success of the BJP in Gujarat provided a model for the party's expansion elsewhere, though there remains some grumbling from RSS ranks over this tactic as well as concerns regarding the development of a cult of personality around the charismatic and popular Modi.

Modi's transition from the RSS to the BJP in 1987 resulted not only in his bringing a new model of campaigning that led to the expansion of the party's social base, but after he became the chief minister of Gujarat in 2001, he brought fresh ideas on how to improve administration and how to make it more development-oriented to meet the needs of the people. Among his innovations was the establishment of training centres for government employees (and party cadre) to better acquaint them with outstanding issues and the range of possible solutions with the objective of higher economic development. But perhaps even more important was his insistence that his bureaucrats focus on advancing his agenda, especially such large, complex issues as the transformation of India's tax regime and the massive sanitation campaign during his first term.

Another sign of the BJP's success in effective organization was the massive two-day conclave, starting 10 March 2022, in southern Gujarat, which brought together some 30,000 senior local figures from the government, the bureaucracy and the party. Modi came to this meeting right after his party's excellent showing in the assembly elections. One of Modi's first acts after forming the national government in 2014 had been to organize a similar conclave of senior bureaucrats and elements of the RSS family of organizations for an exchange of views on the issues facing the country. Throughout his political career, economic development has been at the core of his message— and he recognized that this required an efficient organization committed to what he was trying to do. Singh's book closely analyses this process.

There is, in addition, a strong Hindu-oriented ideological undercurrent to Modi's views which he might have judged necessary to build national cohesion in a country as diverse as India, with its dozens of languages, myriad castes, based at least theoretically on a hierarchic base and on the wide differences in income levels. He might also have seen this as a means to mobilizing support from a largely religious population in a way that crosses caste, class and other barriers. Yet it almost certainly also reflects Modi's personal views as well. In Modi's late teens, there was a clash between family obligations and his commitment to the nation. In opposition to his family's desire that he get a higher education to prepare for a good job (presumably, a steady government job), he decided midway through his college to travel around India, visit shrines and figures known for their religious wisdom, and discover a purpose in life. In line with this commitment, Modi, as an eighteen-year-old groom, never consummated his family-arranged marriage, discovering instead a higher calling of national service. Consistent with this goal, at age twenty-one, following his national pilgrimage, he decided in 1971 to work full time in the RSS. Based on his capable execution of tasks and his devotion to the RSS, he was selected as a full-time *pracharak* a year later and took part in the first two RSS officer training sessions to immerse himself in the organization's ideology and thus check the boxes expected of a successful RSS worker.*

When the young Modi went on his national pilgrimage, his goal was a kind of spiritual enlightenment. He visited religious institutions and developed a relationship with their leaders. Among the first was a visit to Kolkata's Belur Math, the headquarters of the influential Ramakrishna Mission, founded by Swami Vivekananda. He seriously considered becoming a contemplative monk but, on the advice of its monks, abandoned this idea for the worldly activism of its founder, whose core message was, 'Service to man is service to God,' which resonates favourably in the RSS.

Reports about the young Modi indicate that organizing came rather naturally to him. He reportedly took a lead in organizing other boys, whatever their caste or religion, in a range of activities. Among those activities was acting in plays, a role that introduced him to the power of words. He was also impressed by the cultural symbolism of Hinduism and came eventually to see in it the roots of national unity. This recognition led him to the RSS, which espouses a very similar message.

Modi's demonstrated organizational skills were reflected in his steady rise in the RSS, after he dedicated himself to the RSS at age twenty-one and soon after was formally selected as a full-time worker pracharak. The ideological Hindu core informing Prime Minister Modi's views has been witnessed dramatically since the start of his second term in 2019, in his advocacy of moves to build a temple to Lord Ram, perhaps the

---

* Modi later received a Bachelor of Arts in political science from the School of Open Learning of Delhi University in 1978. In 1983, he received an MA in political science from Gujarat University.

most popular Hindu deity in much of India. Modi—a member of a low-caste group referred to by sociologists as OBC (Other Backward Classes)—personally led the ground-laying ceremony and, in a reversal of the caste hierarchy, had Brahmin priests assisting him. Also assisting him was the monk chief minister of Uttar Pradesh, Yogi Adityanath. Similar religiously infused rituals were performed at the religious centre of Varanasi (a city which Modi represents in Parliament), where he, in late 2021, led the inauguration ceremony of a lane from the renowned Kashi Vishwanath Temple (dedicated to Lord Shiva) to the Ganges. He even performed the ceremonial dip in the sacred Ganges, dressed in saffron robes. Major television channels and national newspapers lavished attention on these events. With state election looming in Uttar Pradesh, press reports covering these ceremonies helped build popular support for Modi and, by extension, for his party.

Singh notes that Modi moved on his Hindutva agenda prompted, perhaps, by the impressive popular support for him in his second term. Besides the temple issues noted above, he proposed a law to outlaw 'triple talaq' (a practice in the Muslim community whereby a husband could instantly divorce his wife), which many commentators saw as a first step towards a uniform civil code applicable to families of all faiths—a long-time Hindutva plank. Then came the resolution to revoke special status to the Muslim-majority state of Jammu and Kashmir. Third came the parliamentary amendment to the Citizenship Act, which granted legal status to migrants from other South Asian countries who had fled from persecution before 2014, but excluded Muslims. Then came the temple efforts noted above that further provided a statement about the place of religion and Hindu culture in Modi's vision of India.

There is still another significant temple issue that is raised by many Hindus: the Krishna Janmasthan temple in Mathura (also in Uttar Pradesh), which, like the Ram temple, is held by many religious Hindus to be the spot where a senior divinity (in this case, Krishna) took human form and on which an Islamic structure (the Shahi Eidgah) replaced a Krishna temple by order of Emperor Aurangzeb in the late seventeenth century. The dispute revolves around proposals to build the Janmasthan temple, which would of course require the demolition of the existing Shahi Eidgah structure. This issue is complicated by an act of parliament, the Places of Worship (Special Provisions) Act, 1991, that prohibits the conversion to another religion of any religious structure as it stood on 15 August 1947, the day of India's independence. Modi might want to see the results of the 2024 parliamentary vote before deciding how to handle this contentious issue, as it would bring into question India's secular credentials. But his continuing popularity presents the RSS, always suspicious of an individual more powerful than the organization, with a dilemma on how to deal with Modi.

Several senior RSS figures have voiced their misgivings regarding how Modi will use his power and popularity. These concerns could come to the surface following the 2024 parliamentary election, should Modi, who will then be seventy-four, decide to assume the prime ministership for another five-year term. He has said that one should consider retiring from politics at age seventy-five, and the average age of his cabinet is fifty-eight, down from sixty-one in the previous cabinet.* This issue is complicated, as Modi does not seem to be training a successor, and this includes his closest confidant, Amit Shah, who is several years his junior. The victorious 2022 assembly election in Uttar Pradesh put its relatively young chief minister,

---

* Most retirements in India are somewhere between ages of sixty and sixty-five. The seventy-five-year rule has generally been followed in the BJP and the RSS, though there are some exceptions. The head of the RSS will himself be seventy-five in 2025. Both he and Modi are in good health.

Yogi Adityanath, in a position to be considered an eventual successor. While Yogi, now in his second term, has proved his policy credentials by focusing on popular issues like law and order, welfare schemes and job-creation, as well as demonstrated his voter-mobilization skills, the liability is his lack of an RSS background and his disconnect from the advantages of its social networks.

Over the past ten years, with the assistance of Amit Shah, Modi has centralized power both within the party and within the bureaucracy. There is no real opposition to him within the BJP or within the larger RSS family of organizations. The former national alternative, the Congress party, is disintegrating, and the opposition, filled with jealous regional barons, seems unable to work together. He is the strong man at the helm of the state that many Indians find compatible with good governance and regard as a symbol of the country's national identity. Some have marvelled at his 'Teflon' ability to survive mistakes and social problems, because many Indians believe he genuinely works for their welfare and also backs the Hindu cultural world accepted by most Indians.

Take the recent state assembly election in Uttar Pradesh, where the BJP won 255 of 403 seats (273 seats counting two small allies) and secured a majority on its own for the second time in a row, even though it had faced multiple COVID surges, massive farmers' protests against a legislation favouring market mechanisms and significant unemployment. Though it returned to power with a reduced majority from the 2017 polls, it almost had a 3 per cent vote growth (to about 42 per cent) in 2022. The results seem to support Singh's idea that the 'Modi–Shah duo has perfected the art of micromanagement of elections'.

This electoral project also had an ideological vision: an effort to, as Singh notes, replace the 'Congress system . . .

conceived by [a] Western-educated elite' with a BJP that is 'the sole contender for the claim of a wholly Indian, home-grown way of party-building'. The question is whether this project will continue after Modi. Singh thinks it will, as Modi will likely leave behind a robust organization closely coordinating with the people on the one side and the government/bureaucracy on the other.

Walter Andersen,
Author, and former head of South Asia Studies,
School of Advanced International Studies,
Johns Hopkins University, USA

Introduction

A Lifetime of Organizing. And More Organizing. Forever Organizing.

'Sangha Shakti Kaliyuge' is the motto often found inscribed in the buildings that run the activities of the Rashtriya Swayamsevak Sangh (RSS). As the motto connotes, the founding principle of the RSS lays emphasis on the collectivity of society and the building up of a *rashtra*, nation, as a corporal entity. At the *shakhas*, or the morning drills conducted by RSS volunteers, all across the country, this training inculcates a sense of discipline and organizing skills among volunteers. They play games, sing in chorus and take the collective vow to protect the motherland, which they address as 'Maa Bharti', or Mother India.

As the RSS and its affiliates have grown in size and influence, there have been many scholarly books dealing with this organic growth and dynamics that have influenced the course of Indian politics. This book is focused exclusively on the organizational skills of one individual: Narendra Damodardas Modi. I first heard about him when a superintendent of police in Uttar Pradesh (UP), who was escorting the then BJP president Murli Manohar Joshi's Ekta Yatra (1990–91) through the state, said in a tone that carried a mix of awe and incredulity, 'There is someone called Narendra Modi who is managing this yatra in an extraordinary manner.' Though Uttar Pradesh was then ruled by the BJP, with Kalyan Singh as chief minister, the police escort team had found it difficult to penetrate the inner security ring of Joshi's cavalcade. 'Their volunteers are daredevils and drive their Maruti vans in such a manner that it is next to impossible to come near the vehicle carrying Joshi,' the police superintendent said.

The manner in which he organized the Ekta Yatra bowled over the security agencies in Uttar Pradesh. His micromanagement and hands-on approach galvanized the army of volunteers, who delivered with clockwork precision. Those driving the vans along with the vehicle carrying Joshi were trained to catch recorded instructions on audio tapes on the move and pass it on to the others, to keep everyone on the same page. Volunteers carried fax machines (those were the pre-Internet days) to remain in touch with party offices and media outlets.

What I heard from police officers of UP in 1991 gave me a fair impression of Modi as a highly organized and efficient leader. Though I had not met him, I knew about his traits through sources. It so happened that I moved to Delhi in 1995, when I quit as special correspondent of the *Telegraph* in Lucknow and joined the *Pioneer* in the national capital. In my first assignment there as a reporter covering the BJP beat, I ran into Modi at the party's national executive meeting at the Parliament Annexe. During an afternoon session, I saw him walking towards the main hall, virtually accosted him in the typical reporter style and introduced myself. That was the time when Modi was literally exiled from his home state, Gujarat, and posted in Delhi in order to stave off the factional war within the party, after Shankersinh Vaghela's revolt against Chief Minister Keshubhai Patel. Modi would have been in low spirits after being shunted out, but he took this change in his stride and was focused on the task ahead.

He was assigned the onerous task of building the party's base in Haryana, Punjab and Himachal Pradesh. Though the BJP had a strong presence in Himachal Pradesh and had an alliance with the Akali Dal in Punjab, it faced a daunting challenge in Haryana, where it was marginalized by regional satraps like Bansi Lal and Om Prakash Chautala. The social fault lines along caste identities ran too deep in Haryana—which was carved out of Punjab following the division of the state on the basis of language—and it appeared next to impossible to overcome this problem.

Modi goaded the state leadership to prepare a composite strategy with short-term objectives and long-term goals. He successfully sewed up an alliance with Bansi Lal in the first stage and enabled the party to become a partner in the ruling coalition headed by the stalwart. But this experiment did not last long, as the BJP soon fell out with Bansi Lal. It then tried an alliance with Chautala, which, too, did not work.

The experiment with coalition politics is indeed a side story. What was really significant was the base Modi built in the state and how he projected the BJP as an alternative political force. In district after district, he mobilized cadres and disabused them of the notion that caste was the only factor that drove the politics of the state. He came up with out-of-the-box ideas, like fielding a Kargil war martyr's widow, Sudha Yadav, in Lok Sabha election, even though sections of the party had opposed the move. Similarly, he asked the party's state unit leaders to rope in young people from diverse social backgrounds and train them in party work. He insisted on building infrastructure—he wanted the party to have its own offices—pushed for computerization and held training sessions for newcomers. The majority of them were not steeped in the culture and values imbibed from the RSS shakhas, but the discipline and values were inculcated in them by making them undergo a series of training sessions. In Modi's view, training is a science which helps mould people's minds, and it is an essential ingredient in building an organization.

Modi's work in Haryana had a long gestation period—it did not bear fruit initially, but his efforts came good in the assembly election of 2014, when the BJP won a clear mandate. Modi, as is his wont, ignored the supposed relevance of caste

and chose a Punjabi Khatri, Manohar Lal Khattar, as the chief
minister. The choice did come as a surprise but conformed to
a pattern. Modi believes in turning conventional wisdom on its
head. He does it with a carefully planned strategy and not for
the heck of it.

In adjacent Himachal Pradesh, Modi displayed similar traits
as an organizer and expanded the party in a phenomenal manner.
But in contrast to Haryana, Himachal Pradesh was a propitious
ground for the BJP. The state primarily runs on a two-party
system in which the BJP or its earlier version, the Bharatiya
Jana Sangh (BJS), is ranged against the Congress. After the
Emergency, Shanta Kumar emerged as the undisputed leader in
the state—he was of the newly formed Janata Party into which
the BJS had merged its identity. Shanta Kumar became the
first non-Congress chief minister of the state and continued till
1980, when he was toppled by the Congress. In the wake of the
Ayodhya campaign hitting its prime, after L.K. Advani's Rath
Yatra, the BJP bounced back, and Shanta Kumar was again
chosen as the chief minister. But his term abruptly came to an
end: after the demolition of the Babri mosque in Ayodhya on
6 December 1992, the P.V. Narasimha Rao government sacked
the BJP governments in Uttar Pradesh, Himachal Pradesh,
Rajasthan and Madhya Pradesh, and imposed President's rule
in these states.

Much before Modi arrived on the scene in Himachal
Pradesh, Shanta Kumar was the tallest leader there. He was
known to be close to Atal Bihari Vajpayee and Advani, then
the most influential duo of the BJP. Modi toured all across the
state and soon realized that any status quo in the leadership
would only limit the party's growth. He started roping in
and promoting a group of youngsters to expand the party's
base—much to the annoyance of the old guard. For instance,
in Haryana, he insisted on developing infrastructure for the

party and persuaded the state unit to buy land and build its own offices in all districts. In order to expedite the work, Modi planned his visits to various districts in such a way as to be able to stay in the district headquarters of the party. In these offices, he introduced computers and later the Internet, to keep a record of the party's programmes and cadre strength, and to connect with people from other parts of the state.

Initially, such corporate-like moves in politics evoked scepticism but became a part of the routine after some time. He filled the leadership vacuum by mobilizing district-level leaders to the state level and asked them to camp in other areas. In one stroke, he built a team of leaders in Himachal Pradesh who developed their individual identity in the state. One such leader was Prem Kumar Dhumal, who emerged as an alternative to Shanta Kumar in his own right. In the state assembly election of 1998, when the BJP and the Congress won thirty-one seats each out of the sixty-eight, there was a strong possibility of the Congress cobbling together the majority. Modi, however, strategized to outmanoeuvre the Congress in a carefully planned operation. He roped in the much-maligned Sukh Ram and formed the government. The BJP government led by Dhumal lasted for the full five-year term for the first time. (Modi's methodology is discussed in detail in Chapter 2.)

His mission in the northern states completed, Modi assumed charge as the general secretary (organization) of the BJP at the national level and took up more responsibilities, which included maintaining smooth and healthy relations between the party and the coalition government led by it. There were reports of friction between the government and a section of the party's organizational leadership, within the RSS and the Swadeshi Jagaran Manch (SJM). Modi maintained a delicate balance and continued to expand the organization by holding training sessions and roping in the youth. The most challenging task he undertook was the expansion of the party in Madhya Pradesh, a state where the party had deep roots as it was the political cradle of some of its tallest leaders—Vajpayee, Vijaya Raje Scindia, Kailash Joshi, Sunder Lal Patwa and Vikram Varma, to name a few. At the organizational level, Madhya Pradesh's state unit was built by Kushabhau Thakre, who knew Madhya Pradesh like the back of his hand. There are many legends abound about his organizational skills. An amiable and mild-mannered leader, Thakre was quite a contrast to his namesake in Maharashtra. Coming from the RSS background, Thakre was in the mould of a textbook Sangathanist leader. There is no denying the fact that he built the party's cadre in Madhya Pradesh by the sweat of his brow. He played mentor to all the stalwart leaders of the state.

Modi took up this assignment at a critical juncture, when Madhya Pradesh was to be bifurcated after the 1998 state assembly election. Nobody knew it better than him that the task was really unenviable. Here, he displayed his skills, building on the work Thakre had done and also innovating. At the same time, he propped up a new leadership in Madhya Pradesh and Chhattisgarh, the region that would become a separate state, much to the annoyance of the old guard. He coined the slogan, 'Ek vote mein do pradesh (Win two states by giving one vote to the BJP).' Chief Minister Digvijaya Singh of the Congress, fighting for a second stint, had gained popularity on account of his dogged pursuance of various social welfare schemes. He was shrewd enough to escape the landmine of the bifurcation issue and endorsed the formation of Chhattisgarh. The BJP mobilized its cadre but could not effectively emerge as an alternative due to the bickering among its state leadership. Though Digvijaya Singh won the assembly election, the organizational activity by Modi laid a solid foundation for the emergence of a younger generation of leadership, which included Raman Singh, Uma Bharti and Shivraj Singh Chauhan.

The transition to the next generation of leadership was carried out in a seamless manner when the subsequent assembly elections were held in Madhya Pradesh and Chhattisgarh. Since then, Madhya Pradesh and Chhattisgarh have remained impregnable bastions of the BJP. The party's organizational strength has grown by leaps and bounds. Modi's strategy of expanding the party was quite at variance with the traditional Sangathanist mode of Kushabhau Thakre, who exclusively insisted on roping in those who were quite immersed in the ethos of the RSS, preferably the *swayamsevaks*. Modi's strategy was twofold: he primarily persisted with the Sangathanist model to build the superstructure of the organization but also relied on influential outsiders or notable personalities who could fetch votes. He did not lose sight of leaders whose charm could be an influencing factor.

In his capacity as the general secretary (organization) of the party at the national level, Modi evolved his own style for organizational expansion, which, though aligned with the RSS's worldview, had three distinctly different tactics. He followed the basic guideline of the Sangathanist model and allowed the organization to be guided by full-time workers loaned from the RSS. But he also relied on the inclusion of 'notables' from outside the saffron fold in order to appeal to a wider audience. He apparently borrowed this concept from the Congress, which had expanded its base by roping in eminent persons from different walks of life and reached out to a large audience. Historically, the BJP and its forerunner, the BJS, had strong reservations about the inclusion of notables—the process has come to be known as the 'notabalization of the party'. Old stalwarts of the party drawn from the RSS flock felt that such a process would degenerate the BJP and make it look like the

Congress. In the perception of leaders of the saffron fold, the Congress symbolized all the evils that plagued Indian politics. Modi realized rather too soon that though this diagnosis was correct, it would severely limit the BJP's growth if scepticism about the inclusion of notables continued.

Modi discarded this diffidence, and his efforts got the approval of Vajpayee and Advani, as both shared the same view. In fact, they were instrumental in bringing many eminent non-political personalities and celebrities into the BJP's fold. Some of them were known to have been highly critical of the Sangh Parivar in the past. Along with these two tactics to promote the growth of the party, in course of time Modi realized the huge potential of a popular leader. With his rich understanding of the Indian masses during his wandering years in quest of spirituality and as a whole-timer in the RSS, Modi discovered that a leader would gain popularity and people's trust if he became a symbol of their aspirations. Given India's historical context, he surmised that those exuding tactful strength have always caught people's imagination. Later in his stint as Gujarat's chief minister, Modi employed all three tactics, which led to phenomenal growth of the party and made Gujarat an electoral fortress for it. The Congress, despite its strong base in the state, gradually found itself in a perpetually debilitating position.

Modi moved to Gujarat in 2001 as chief minister in a delicate situation. There were reports of corruption and misgovernance in the state, following the massive earthquake on 26 January 2001 that affected the Kachchh region in particular. The Keshubhai Patel government was at the receiving end for its inability to contain corruption in the relief and rehabilitation work. Keshubhai was perceived to have lost touch with reality because of his ill health, and the allegation gained traction that he was surrounded by a coterie that thrived on corruption. Though none of these allegations could be proven, the perception had dented the image of the BJP. Modi was parachuted into Gujarat to salvage the BJP's bruised image ahead of the state election due next year. Though he had a profound understanding of society, politics and organization, Modi didn't have any experience of running the government. While learning the ropes of governance, he was saddled with the responsibility of rejuvenating the party which appeared to be in a bad shape not only in terms of organization but also in terms of motivation. Since Modi was then essentially an organization man, he had to make a determined attempt to acquaint himself with governance. It was indeed a tough task. And thus began the evolution of Modi the organizer into Modi the administrator.

Those who have worked with him describe him as an avid learner. He understood right from the word go that governance is a complex issue. He started giving a patient hearing to all the top bureaucrats before arriving at his decisions. Once he called one of his senior officers to learn from him how to read a file and make notes in it. It did not take long for him to realize that the bureaucracy and the entire state machinery were ill-equipped and demotivated to face the challenge of reconnecting with the people. Gujarat was then reeling under a series of reverses. A long spell of drought followed by a massive earthquake had shattered people's confidence, and the government machinery was in disarray on account of an uninspiring political leadership.

Modi as an organization man, with his deep understanding of the state's social psychology, laid out a strategy to bring the government's plans in sync with the people's aspirations. He was temporarily disrupted in this campaign due to the Godhra train-burning incident in February 2002 and its aftermath. Gujarat's image was sullied substantially, and Modi, being a former pracharak groomed in the RSS's values, became the central target for those who saw him as a challenge to 'secularism' and 'the idea of India'. Modi assiduously avoided confronting his critics and started building Brand Gujarat for his future political project. (This is analysed in detail in Chapter 3.) But what was simply outstanding was the manner in which he mobilized the state machinery in sync with the party's cadre to achieve his political objectives.

Contrary to the general impression, Gujarat was never an easy state for the Sangh Parivar to hold. Innuendos about the involvement of the RSS in Mahatma Gandhi's assassination had virtually created a schism between the Sangh Parivar's ideology and the people of the state. Like other constituents of the Sangh Parivar, the BJP was regarded as out of sync with the people's values. It was primarily considered an urban-centric phenomenon. Modi had liaised with the BJP even when he was a pracharak and devised innovative methods to expand the party's growth. In the process, he realized the sociological limitations of the BJP and the inability of the organization to find resonance among the masses. His transition from the RSS to the BJP in 1987 and his onward political journey are indeed instructive. He pushed the party on to a trajectory from where its social base continues to expand.

During his stint as the chief minister of Gujarat, Modi evolved not only as an administrator but also as an organizer. His ability to dovetail government initiatives with the party programmes helped him to put together an innovative strategy to substantially occupy people's mind space. Herein lay Modi's strategic astuteness in evolving a 'Gujarat model', which was different from the traditional model of the BJP. He built a committed cadre of workers across the state from various social strata. In order to bring the new workers in sync with the traditional Sangh leadership, he organized training camps all across the state. 'Training is a science,' Modi would tell his close aides. That was why training camps for party cadres and even government employees became a regular feature in Gujarat. During his thirteen-year stint as chief minister, Gujarat evolved as a role model that inspired awe across India. By winning three successive assembly elections, in 2002, 2007 and 2012, he refuted the belief that good governance is bad politics. This laid the ground for his political journey at the national level.

As the 2014 Lok Sabha election drew near, Modi emerged as the new hope after a decade of Manmohan Singh's government, which was seen as effete and corrupt in popular perception. Though Manmohan Singh was the prime minister, he hardly got recognition as a leader in his party. He was at best seen as a retainer of 10 Janpath, the official residence of the Congress president, Sonia Gandhi. In sharp contrast, Modi epitomized a masculine leadership. But his ascendance faced stiff challenges from within and outside. Within the party, he found obstacles but overcame them without difficulty. Still, there were genuine doubts if he would be able to win the support of people across the country. At the same time, the baggage of the 2002 riots was held against him by the liberals and secularists who were part of the NDA. Bihar chief minister Nitish Kumar rose in revolt and parted ways with the National Democratic Alliance (NDA) led by the BJP.

In the run-up to the 2014 election, there was a degree of doubt over the efficacy of projecting Modi as the prime ministerial candidate. Would it be wise to project an individual over the party? Of course, there was a considered view within the Sangh Parivar that Modi's individual charm had assumed larger-than-life proportions and that the party should use it to its advantage. There is no doubt that Modi left nothing to chance to turn the situation to his favour. The BJP's resounding victory in 2014 was as much a testimony to his exceptional organizational skills as to his charismatic personality that charmed the electorate.

The victory also busted many myths about the BJP. One, that it was a party with only upper-caste and urban-centric support base. Second, that it faced limitations when it came to growing beyond the 'cow belt'. Third, that the party would not be able to overcome the challenge in states where regional players were powerful. The results proved beyond doubt that the BJP had transcended caste boundaries and the urban–rural divide to find acceptance among voters. Though the party grew in size in the southern, eastern and North-eastern states, its access to these regions was not easy. The Lok Sabha election in 2014 clearly underlined the party's strengths and vulnerabilities in these places. The party leadership wasted no time to focus on addressing the vulnerabilities and dispelling any complacency among the cadres in the stronger areas.

When party president Rajnath Singh became the home minister in the Modi government, Amit Shah was chosen as his replacement. Shah, who'd had a long association with Modi in Gujarat, launched a vigorous attempt to align the party's programmes with the government's ambitious schemes—a model extended from Gujarat. The BJP's predominant position as the principal pole of Indian politics was unambiguously established in a series of state assembly polls across the country. Circumstances also favoured the BJP following the switching of sides by Nitish Kumar and factional feuds in Tamil Nadu arising out of J. Jayalalithaa's death.

With Modi's prime ministership, the BJP has acquired the role that the Congress had played for long decades after Independence. This dramatic change did not come about in a day. The Sangh Parivar has been consistently striving to get a powerful political space, but the story of Modi's rise and his organizational skills is a crucial chapter in the political history of the country, as he was instrumental in realizing what had once appeared impossible.

Much is written about Modi's politics and ideology. It is naively assumed that his rise has solely to do with Hindutva plus economic development—often called 'Moditva'. But this view ignores the methods he deployed to broaden the base of his organization, the BJP, and helped to connect it with more and more people. His ways are often old textbook methods, applied with more tenacity and conviction, and even his rivals have started imitating his innovations, albeit unwittingly. A journalistic narration and documentation of his eclectic ways of party-building will be useful not only to practitioners but also to scholars. Much of what I have written here is based on interviews and my reading of recorded history. My own experience as a reporter who covered the events that led to the present political situation was also helpful in narrating this story of one of India's most exciting political journeys.

1

A Flood | A Riot | A Rath Yatra
The First Sightings of an Organizer
(1986–95)

Often great political turns begin with apolitical events. They escape the attention of political historians. Gujarat was once the Congress party's bastion, and since the mid-1990s the BJP has been in power in the state, with virtually no challenge from the opposition. How did this turn come about? Two events, not much talked about in this context, laid the foundation for a new politics in Gujarat.

On 11 August 1979, Morbi town in Saurashtra, known as the manufacturing hub for pottery and wall clocks, was flooded out after the nearby dam on the Machchhu River broke. In what is described as the biggest dam-burst tragedy in history, up to 25,000 people died as the whole town went under water. It was later established that this was a man-made disaster, and timely intervention could have averted the tragedy. The irrigation minister was Keshubhai Patel, an RSS veteran and part of the Janata Party government led by Babubhai Jashbhai Patel, in parallel to the experiment at the national level in which the Bharatiya Jana Sangh (BJS) had merged into the Janata Party. Keshubhai rushed to the spot only to beat a hasty retreat as the rising tide was a threat to his safety as well. The government had been paralysed for long before relief measures were initiated. Various social organizations were roped in to mitigate the people's plight.

What appears to have stood out in this relief operation was the focused approach of a team of RSS volunteers led by a young pracharak (full-timer) known as Narendra Damodardas Modi. When the dam broke, Modi was in Chennai along with Nanaji Deshmukh of the Deendayal Research Institute (DRI), an autonomous body affiliated to the RSS. On hearing the news of the large-scale destruction, he immediately rushed back to Gujarat and organized the relief operations. Unlike the confusion and chaos that often characterize relief operations, the assistance by RSS volunteers was quite methodical and clinical. Areas that were adopted by these volunteers saw rehabilitation of the victims at quite a rapid pace as they started picking up the threads of their lives. Notably, some of these localities had substantial Muslim population too.

In 1979, Gujarat, along with the rest of the country, was in an anti-Indira mood, yet the alternative to the Congress it banked on was a replica of the Congress. With Morarji Desai, a long-time Congress man, as the prime minister, the secular–socialist–centrist political formation, the Janata Party, was the main political force. Having merged into it, the BJS, the RSS-inspired political affiliate, had lost its identity. In such a political context, the RSS cadre found new social acceptance among the people of Gujarat during the Machchhu dam crisis. This change in perception was welcome for the organization, as people at large had perceived it with suspicious eyes, given its rumoured involvement in the assassination of Mahatma Gandhi and the subsequent stigma of a ban. The dedication and commitment its volunteers had showed in reaching out to the needy after the dam disaster revealed a new face of the organization to the people of Gujarat.

This was hardly an isolated incident. It needs to be seen in the context of another incident five years later, in 1984, to get the complete picture. Farmers had launched a movement across the state, known simply as 'Khedu', to protest against the rules that barred them from freely trading their produce outside the state and thus get the best returns. Take the case of jeera, or cumin seed. Its largest market was in Unjha in north Gujarat. Jalore, in neighbouring Rajasthan, not far from Unjha, was one of its largest producers. Farmers on both sides were unhappy as any trade between the two had to negotiate a maze of cumbersome bureaucratic procedures. Needless to say, it enabled corruption in the bureaucracy and meant humiliation for the farmers. The issue had been simmering for long, but both the state and Central governments had paid no attention to it.

This matter was taken up by the Bharatiya Kisan Sangh (BKS), an organization set up in the post-Emergency phase to work for the cause of farmers. It was headed by Dattopant Thengadi, an RSS pracharak who had earned the reputation of being a formidable organizer, having successfully helmed and established a powerful trade union, the Bharatiya Mazdoor Sangh (BMS), aligned with the Sangh Parivar's ideology. Thengadi was quite peeved at the bureaucratic apathy to farmers' plight and was determined to launch a campaign against it. In Rajasthan he roped in an RSS pracharak, Om Mathur, to mobilize farmers, while in Gujarat Modi played the most critical role of planning every minute detail of the agitation from behind the curtain. In the two tumultuous years, 1983–84, the Kisan Sangh units of the two states got together and urged farmers to sell their produce in cross-border markets without going through the corrupt and harassing bureaucratic processes. Farmers decided to break the law in the same way as Mahatma Gandhi had broken the law by making salt.

With an emphasis on Gandhi's symbolism, the Kisan Sangh planned a massive rally on 2 October 1984 in Ahmedabad. More than 1 lakh farmers gathered there to protest against the government's policies. The movement had captured people's imagination in rural areas. It had also brought to the fore rural distress and the government's apathy towards farmers. The anger exploded on the streets as farmers fought pitched battles with the police. In the police action, some farmers were killed and scores were injured. Modi asked the cadres to seek donations from people across the state to put together a fund to support the families of those who had died in the police firing. This was a unique way of urging other people to support the cause of the farmers while also retaining the farmers' stakes in the movement. The Khedu movement went on to create a committed cadre for the BKS, which later developed a strong base in the state's agrarian society. For the first time, the movement expanded the Sangh Parivar's base in the rural areas of Gujarat and effectively enhanced its social acceptability, which was otherwise limited in the state. The symbolism of Gandhi in the peasants' movement was deliberately appropriated to exorcise the ghost of Gandhi's assassination that had got stuck with the RSS.

These two events, within a span of five years, were quite critical in building a base for the Sangh Parivar and ultimately benefitting its political affiliate, the BJP. This formed the backdrop of Modi's transition from the RSS to the BJP in 1986–87. But the transition was not without its hiccups. The BJP, formed in 1980 after the disintegration of the Janata Party, was decimated in the 1984 general election, winning only two seats in the Lok Sabha. The morale of the party's cadre was at its lowest. Meanwhile, in Gujarat, particularly in Ahmedabad and Surat, communal riots had become a recurring feature in the 1980s. Fear was in the air, and a palpable sense of insecurity prevailed, especially among those living in areas of mixed population of Hindus and Muslims. Much of the blame for creating this atmosphere of fear and violence went to the new political idiom of 'KHAM', invented by an astute Congress politician, the then chief minister Madhavsinh Solanki. KHAM stood for Kshatriya, Harijan, Adivasi and Muslim. Though this social coalition was indeed a winning combination for the Congress in the state, Solanki's victory in 1980 had engendered an unbridled hubris among Congress workers. This once again exposed the social fault lines as the Patidars, who form nearly 18 per cent of the population in the state, rose in revolt against the state's new policy to extend reservation benefits to more communities within the KHAM camp. The urban upper middle class came out in the streets in protest in 1982 and again in 1985, but the anti-reservation movement was handled so ineptly by the Solanki government that it turned into large-scale communal riots that continued for over six months. Bootleggers close to Solanki had a field day, and some of the walled city localities of Ahmedabad faced curfew for months on end. The anarchy came to an end only when Solanki was replaced with his home minister, Amarsinh Chaudhary. The state had been polarized along caste and communal lines.

Such were the turbulent times in which Modi's transition into a political role took place. Ahmedabad was the most volatile city in Gujarat. There was a saying among the Hindus in Ahmedabad that went as, 'You [the Congress] can win Delhi but not Ahmedabad.' The implicit meaning was that the ruling party was partisan, favouring the minorities, and the Hindus of Ahmedabad would teach it a lesson. The atmosphere of polarization became quite pronounced in the city and elsewhere ahead of the 1987 civic body elections of the four major corporations of the state—Ahmedabad, Surat, Vadodara and Rajkot.

Chaudhary, the new chief minister, did not help matters when he banned the Jagannath Yatra, an annual ceremony that began in the nineteenth century and is among the principal events in the city's religious–cultural calendar. The move was apparently necessitated for security reasons, as the religious procession would pass through many mixed-population localities, leading sometimes to communal clashes. But it was also seen as an affront to the Hindus and their religious traditions. It proved to be the ultimate provocation for the devout Hindus of the walled city and elsewhere. Given the past history of communal violence and the impression that the Chaudhary government was bent upon pandering to the Muslims, the issue had been gradually snowballing into a confrontation between the Hindus and the government. The Sangh Parivar had thrown in its lot with the Hindus.

The yatra, a local counterpart to the more famous chariot procession taken out in Puri, Odisha, begins from the Lord Jagannath temple and proceeds around the walled city, including pockets of Muslim population. In peaceful times, the yatra gets a rousing reception from Muslims—an expression of respect for Hindu religious sentiments. But things had changed over the years following the series of communal riots in the 1980s and the emergence of a powerful Muslim underworld under the leadership of a gangster called Abdul Lateef. This underworld was seen as enjoying the patronage of successive Congress regimes.

In 1986, when the yatra ban controversy erupted, Modi had still not made full transition from the RSS into the BJP. Though he was active in the functioning of the RSS–BJP and their affiliates, he was still working behind the scenes. Meanwhile, tension mounted in the walled city as the yatra day approached. Policemen were posted all around the temple to prevent any move to take out the procession. A message was circulated all around the city that Hindus were determined to defy the ban and take out the Yatra. A group of trained volunteers had also parked themselves inside the temple the night before. In the morning, as people made their daily visit to the hundreds of milk booths, they got the message that the yatra was to begin soon, come what may. This message was meant only to generate wider social legitimacy for the defiance of the state's order.

In the morning, the Jagannath temple resembled a police camp, and one of the elephants—they are housed in the temple complex round the year and lead the annual procession—surprised all as it led the charge and broke open the police barrier. Within a minute, all police arrangements were thrown out of gear, and before anyone could realize what was happening the Rath Yatra had started. Since big elephants with trained mahouts were leading the charge, the policemen, having run helter-skelter, rearranged themselves and provided a security cordon to the yatra. While passing through sensitive areas of mixed population, the yatra did trigger clashes, but the large contingent of police personnel took it upon themselves to remove the hurdles in its way. People of Ahmedabad still remember it as the 'Swayambhoo Yatra', a procession that proceeded on its own.

But of course, it did not happen 'on its own', and the elephant did not plan to defy the government order. There was a meticulous strategy behind it all. And it was widely attributed to Modi, even if there was never a credible acknowledgment from him. But soon after the yatra, Chief Minister Chaudhary reportedly made inquiries with BJP leaders, including Keshubhai Patel, about this man called Modi. It was with this reputation in political circles that Modi joined the BJP.

Though by June 1986 he had started attending BJP meetings informally alongside his RSS work, he continued his unofficial attachment with the party with the attitude of a learner. It was in February–March 1987 that his work was appreciated within the party and he was made the general secretary (organization) of the BJP's state unit. His first test: the Ahmedabad civic elections in 1987. The elections were held against the backdrop of an atmosphere that was communally charged and made Hindus suspicious of the Congress. This was Modi's first assignment after he formally made the transition into the BJP from the RSS.

The BJP had been a minor player in the Ahmedabad Municipal Corporation (AMC) elections in the past. In 1975, the BJS, the forerunner to the BJP, had won only fourteen seats in alliance with the Congress (O) of Morarji Desai. In 1981, its tally improved to twenty-one. The 1987 elections were critical, as they were expected to lay the foundation on which the BJP could build its future in the state. The elections in 1987 were to be held right after delimitation, which had brought the eastern parts of the city—inhabited largely by migrant labourers, particularly from Uttar Pradesh (UP), Bihar and Madhya Pradesh—into the AMC.

When Modi took charge, the organizational structure of the party was quite nebulous and loose. Though some leaders were popular for their oratory, Modi suspected mere speeches might not get the votes. He roped in leaders like Ashok Bhatt, originally of the Praja Socialist Party (PSP), who, with his firebrand campaign tactics, had become popular in his Khadia municipal ward in the walled city. Modi began mobilizing the party's cadre in right earnest and classified the booths in A, B and C categories: A-category booths were safe places where consolidation needed to be done, while B and C categories required special attention to turn them into A category. Ten party workers were identified to be placed in each booth. Such an elaborate exercise at the organizational level was unprecedented within the BJP. Modi's dogged persistence to restructure the organization to meet the requirement of elections was much frowned upon by senior leaders like Harin Pathak and others who had been winning the municipal elections since 1975.

Meanwhile, Lateef, who saw himself as a sort of Robin Hood for the minorities during the riots, decided to contest the election from five wards as an independent candidate—though he was in jail. His election symbol was lion. While he could not campaign in person, his supporters paraded a caged lion to canvass for the don. With the scars of the recent violence still fresh, this innovative campaign tactic was an attempt to exploit polarization. However, it played in favour of the BJP, which promised to dispel the atmosphere of fear and insecurity among the people of Ahmedabad. The BJP's pro-Hindu inclination was in sharp contrast to the stance of the Congress, which was accused of encouraging criminality in the name of secularism.

Though the BJP seemed to be in the contest, none of the senior party leaders had ever anticipated a victory. At best, they could have visualized a scenario in which the BJP could win the AMC in alliance with the remnants of the Janata Party. This diffidence was not unfounded. In 1971, when Atal Bihari Vajpayee addressed a public rally in Ahmedabad, the BJS had mobilized people in large numbers—it was then billed as the BJS's biggest rally. Yet, in 1972, the party got wiped out in the Lok Sabha election. A succession of defeats, despite apparent rapport with people at times, had driven the state leadership to such cynicism that a victory seemed nearly impossible.

However, a rejuvenated organizational structure and unconventional modes of the party's expansion gave a ray of hope to some party veterans. There was also scope to capitalize on the urban middle-class angst against the Congress that had come out in the open on two counts: the anti-reservation agitations and communal violence. Modi and other decision-makers chose to build on the party's emerging support base by giving tickets to middle-class professionals who were not full-time political workers—schoolteachers, doctors and lawyers.

In February 1987, when the AMC poll results started coming in, the two leading parties were going neck and neck, and a hung house seemed to be on the cards. However, the votes from the wards that were added after delimitation were yet to be counted. Given the impression that non-Gujarati labourers living in the eastern parts were Congress supporters, nobody was expecting a dramatic turnaround in the final numbers. But when the votes were counted, all twenty-one seats went to the BJP. The silent organizational work in this area had paid a rich dividend. The BJP crossed the halfway mark, winning sixty-seven of the 127 seats, while the Congress tally went down to thirty seats. (In the previous election in 1981, the BJP had managed to win only thirteen seats, while the Congress had fifty of the total 105 seats.) What tilted the situation in favour of the BJP was, ironically enough, Lateef's victory in all five wards. He, of course, had to forgo four wards, and here a curious rule of the AMC elections came into play. Instead of fresh elections in such wards, the candidate with the second highest votes was considered the winner. In two of the four wards, the runners-up were BJP candidates, while in the third it was an independent candidate, who declared support to the BJP (one seat went to the Congress)—thus giving the party a clear majority in the house.

The BJP became a serious contender in Gujarat politics, having also won the municipal elections in Surat, Vadodara and Rajkot (where it had had its first-ever victory in the state in 1982). The dramatic turn injected a new vibrancy in the party and dispelled the defeatist mindset of party workers. The Congress strategy of banking on the KHAM support base was no longer invincible. In fact, the BJP was able to forge a more powerful social coalition of the urban middle class and the newly emerging middle class—those who had moved to cities for work and were on the cusp of entering the middle class.

While outsiders gave credit for this success to the party's state president, Shankersinh Vaghela, and the senior-most leader, Keshubhai Patel, the feeling within the party was, as old-timers recalled to me, 'Modi's entry was a good omen'.

In Ahmedabad, the BJP councillors of those times can still recall the day—20 February 1987—when Modi addressed them at the residence of Prahlad Patel, a party leader. He told them that only their good work for people would take them and the party forward. And there was a lot of scope for good work to be done in the AMC, which had been rendered as an ineffective institution in the city's life. Jayendra Pandit, a Brahmin leader roped in from the PSP, was elected as the mayor. For the first time, the AMC took up issues that concerned people. Old-timers recall that immediately after the victory, there was an outbreak of hepatitis in the walled city. The AMC took up cleanliness drives in right earnest and mobilized health workers to create awareness among people about preventive measures.

The AMC also came up with the innovative idea of setting up an electric crematorium and providing free service for funerals. This step touched the lives of the poor, who found it unaffordable to conduct the last rites of their dead in line with traditional Hindu rituals. This move also helped reduce pollution, through the use of electricity instead of wood for the cremations. In yet another instance of connecting with the masses, the AMC opened public parks at night only for girls during the rainy season, for a week or so. This was meant for the young girls who were fasting as part of Gauri Vrat, which also required them to spend the nights without sleeping. They would usually go out late in the evening and take a stroll, but in many densely populated localities there were no public spaces for them and there was the post-riot fear syndrome. The majority of people welcomed the AMC's intervention.

When I spoke to Harin Pathak (who later became a minister of state for home in the Atal Bihari Vajpayee government) and others who served as councillors during that period, they gave credit to Modi for such innovative ideas that found traction among people. In less than a year after the elections, the AMC emerged as a role model for good governance. Though handicapped by financial constraints and hurdles created by the Chaudhary government, its efficient administrative work and sensitivity for people's issues stood out as an exemplary political model that could be replicated elsewhere in the state.

Modi now set his sights on the 1989 general election and the state assembly election of 1990. Having gained substantial experience in mass movements during and since the imposition of the Emergency, and through his behind-the-scenes guiding of protests by various social groups, Modi's understanding of the social psychology in Gujarat was deepening. In the run-up to the 1989 election, V.P. Singh emerged as a crusader against corruption, as the then prime minister, Rajiv Gandhi, faced allegations of corruption in defence deals having to do with Bofors guns and an HDW submarine. The BJP aligned with the Janata Dal, formed from the constituents of the Janata Party and led now by V.P. Singh, to set up a coalition against the Congress. In Gujarat, though the party's central leadership was keen to forge an alliance and contest the election with the Janata Dal, Modi was quite confident of going it alone. His confidence emanated from the preparatory works he had undertaken silently to expand the party's base.

After the AMC victory in 1987, Modi planned to take out a series of rallies all over the state. He began with a Nyaya Yatra, rally for justice, aimed at making people aware of their entitlements when the state was reeling under serious drought conditions. He asked party workers to prepare a *haqpatra*, a list of entitlements, to make farmers aware of their rights. The yatra was planned in such a way as to cover the entire state and ensure that farmers' issues were raised in public meetings. The events provided a platform for a kind of *jansunvai*, a social audit of the government's relief measures.

In the drought-prone state of Gujarat, there was a long tradition of relief interventions from civil society and from voluntary or philanthropic organizations, but this was the first time, under Modi's coordination, that a political party was reaching out to the affected people. This was also the first time a political party was deploying the 'interventionist methodology' to expand its area of influence. In rural areas people were attracted to this endeavour, which was quite innovative in establishing instant rapport with the masses. Apart from creating a mass following, Modi kept mobilizing the cadres and encouraging them perpetually to connect with the people and their issues. Such programmes were planned even at the micro level, down to talukas and panchayats, to keep the cadre always ready.

Among Modi's innovations in the late '80s was the concept of a *chintan baithak*, a brainstorming meet, of the top rung of party leaders, which the party later replicated at the national level. The top twenty-five leaders of the state got together in the Gir forest and spent three days—cut off from the media, without access to telephones and even newspapers—to focus solely on their strategy options. The free and frank discussions acknowledged the party's potential, admitted its weaknesses, touched upon the socio-political conditions and delineated ways to strengthen the cadre.

To institutionalize the Gir experiment, Modi formed a standing 'working group' of 25–30 leaders who started meeting every month to review the activities and plan ahead. This also helped in building team spirit in the leadership. Extending this initiative to the cadre at large was the logical next step. Modi and other leaders launched a series of *abhyasvarga*, or study sessions, across the state, attended by thousands of party workers. The focus was on the party strategy, ideology and the development of the cadre's skills.

Another innovative measure taken by the new general secretary (organization) had to do with the new work culture. Modi believed that office-bearers must not take their office for granted and that each office should have fixed tasks. Some of the seniors might have grumbled at the move, but soon an atmosphere of responsibility and accountability emerged.

No doubt, Modi's methods of the organization and expansion were quite unconventional and at variance with the traditional ways. As Harin Pathak put it, the party knew only the traditional method: hold a public meeting of a well-known leader, who would deliver a speech, and the cadres would mobilize people for an event occasionally. Not without reason, the BJP was then considered a party of the Brahmin–Bania, the two leading upper castes that do not have significant numerical strength in Gujarat. Modi's rigorous method of co-opting the marginalized social groups, the newly emerging ('neo') middle class in urban areas and some 60 lakh non-Gujaratis overstretched the party's resources and caused considerable consternation. But Modi continued with his efforts in his role as the general secretary (organization). Along the way, he was also silently preparing for the crucial 1990 state assembly election, in which he aimed to capture the anti-Congress space.

In the state's politics, the key actor in the anti-Congress space ahead of the state election was Chimanbhai Patel. A shrewd veteran, he was enjoying a second innings after quitting the Congress and joining V.P. Singh's anti-corruption movement. The BJP's central leadership decided to forge an alliance with Chimanbhai and his Janata Dal, and also agreed to his demand for more seats, making the BJP a junior partner. Modi was averse to the alliance as he was confident that the BJP would win on its own.

This confidence was based on his efforts to consolidate the initiatives mentioned before and build the party at the ground level. His micro-management of elections included even coining of catchy slogans that could get traction among the people—a novel move in this party. He discovered a painter and coined a slogan, '*Ab toh bus, BhaJaPa* (Enough! Now it's time for the BJP).' This slogan once again broke the traditional methods of coining long slogans. For a section of voters, it seemed to convey nothing. But Modi realized that the slogan would find resonance with people who were fed up with the successive Congress regimes in the state. At the same time, the slogan emphasized the distinctiveness of the BJP in the political space.

Now he had to prepare the party machinery to fight elections in partnership with Chimanbhai. Though a stalwart of his time, Chimanbhai came to be known as a wily politician and dubiously earned the epithet of 'Chiman Chor' (Chiman the thief) in his previous stint as the chief minister. In such a setting, Modi decided to introduce a new political idiom that could describe the BJP as being distinctively different from other parties.

But this search for a new idiom was just a beginning. Modi was keen to capture the electorate's mind space before the state assembly election in 1990. He planned a state-wide massive mobilization of the BJP cadre in Ahmedabad. All aspirants for assembly seats in the state were asked to come to Ahmedabad in a vehicle decked up as a rath and decorated with party flags and slogans. Hundreds of vehicles improvised as raths did a round of the state for a week and converged in Ahmedabad on the same day. Here, they were given nothing more than a pep talk on how to ensure the expansion of the party's base and win the election.

Insiders say that this massive show of strength was a brilliant strategy to overawe not only the electorate but also potential allies, who, until then, had underestimated the BJP's popularity. Perhaps the BJP could now successfully demand from the Janata Dal a larger share in the seat adjustment? Since Modi was conscious of the fact that the victory in the Lok Sabha would ensure power to V.P. Singh, he substantially focused on the state election and strategized in an effective manner to win maximum seats.

In the Lok Sabha election of 1989, the BJP entered into an alliance with the Janata Dal at the last moment, agreeing to contest twelve seats, vacating the rest fourteen for V.P. Singh's party. Given the anti-Congress mood after the Bofors scandal, V.P. Singh had emerged as a charismatic leader and became the prime minister, but in Gujarat his party won eleven out of fourteen seats, whereas the BJP won all the twelve seats it had contested. (The Congress was reduced to three seats.) The BJP thus emerged as the number one party—all efforts over the years had borne fruit. One of the highlights of the election was the emergence of the party's state president, Shankersinh Vaghela, in the electoral domain. He contested from the Gandhinagar constituency, which includes the state capital as well as affluent sections of Ahmedabad across the river, and won with a wide margin. He would vacate this seat for Advani in 1991, who would make it a prestigious constituency. In the 1991 election, the party would consolidate its grip on the state further by winning twenty seats.

Thus, when the time came for the assembly election, the BJP and Janata Dal were expected to join hands in further decimating the ruling Congress. But the BJP this time was bound to insist on an equal share, if not more. Eventually, the BJP and Janata Dal agreed to contest sixty-eight seats each (out of the 182 seats) in alliance, while keeping their fight in the rest of the seats (forty-six) friendly. Chimanbhai's Janata Dal won seventy seats, with the BJP nearly equal, with sixty-eight seats, and the Congress reduced to thirty-three. Given Chimanbhai's image, there were allegations that the supposed friendly fights were not so friendly and that he had ensured the defeat of some of the BJP candidates. This set the tone for the BJP's relationship with Chimanbhai, which was always marked by suspicion. Yet the government was formed with Chimanbhai as the chief minister and Keshubhai, the tallest party leader at that time, as the deputy chief minister. (This was the first time the state had a deputy CM.) The government couldn't run smoothly for long, as Advani decided to launch his Rath Yatra in September 1990, from Somnath in Gujarat to Ayodhya, to push for the demand for a grand Ram temple there.

The choice of the venue for beginning the yatra put a considerable strain on the ruling alliance. But once again, the BJP decided to stick to its ideological line irrespective of its potential impact on the coalition government. Modi was tasked to make preparations for the Gujarat leg of the yatra. Its route was planned in a way to cover the maximum number of tribal and rural areas, in order to attract those social groups that were not yet associated with the Sangh Parivar. The programmes were chalked out in a manner to get maximum leverage for the party in mobilizing people's opinion and were adequately backed by thousands of committed cadres of the entire Sangh Parivar.

On the day Advani was to begin the yatra, Modi returned to Veraval town near the Somnath temple after mapping the entire route of Advani's mechanized 'chariot'. Those associated with Modi then reveal that he would involve himself in every detail of every event in the course of the yatra, even planning alternative routes should there be any difficulty on the way. There is an interesting anecdote which reveals Modi's attention to detail. A day before the Rath Yatra was to commence, Advani and senior party leader Pramod Mahajan reached Veraval, the major town close to the Somnath temple, and they were a bit dismayed to see no signs of the coming event—no posters and flags in the streets. According to Advani himself, the party was quite sceptical about the success of the Rath Yatra as this was the first mass mobilization programme at the national level. Given that the township had no posters and banners for the yatra, the central leaders were doubtful if there had been adequate preparation to give a leg up to the yatra at its beginning.

When the yatra began the next morning, however, it got a rousing reception, with crowds thronging the way. Modi's team had spread the word effectively after all. These people came from different social segments, including OBC, SC and tribals. In a sense, the BJP had, for the first time, reached out to those sections of society which were beyond the Sangh Parivar's circle of influence.

The overwhelming response to the Gujarat leg of the yatra was as much a surprise for Advani, Mahajan and other leaders as it was for the media persons covering the event. Mahajan was quite alarmed as he had to lead the yatra's next leg through his own state, and now the bar had been set high. 'Don't expect this kind of response in Maharashtra,' he told Advani.

Mahajan argued that the yatra could evoke such a tremendous response all over Gujarat because of the state's peculiar social character, steeped in deep religiosity. What he seemed to have missed initially was the building up of an effective organizational network which had been acting like a well-oiled machine.

There is no denying the fact that the Gujarat leg of the Rath Yatra had set the pace for the rest of India. At the same time, Gujarat managed to reap maximum political benefit from the exercise, which subsumed caste cleavages and coalesced Hindu society in one identity for the first time. Significantly, the Sangh Parivar's organizational network was at the vanguard of this social cohesion, which subsequently turned into a great political advantage. The state found political novelty in these new idioms and culture, offering a different politics and seamlessly aligned with the dominant religious ethos of society.

There was the possibility that once the yatra crossed the state border, the exuberance it generated would die down. But the party's organizational follow-up did not let this happen. The BJP's state unit continued its programmes of mobilizing the cadres and support base at the local level to cement its new-found wider social acceptance. This laid a solid foundation for the party's organizational structure, making it an invincible political force.

Much along the expected lines, the fallout of the yatra once again threw the state into political uncertainty after Advani's arrest in Samastipur, Bihar, on 22 October 1990. The BJP withdrew its support to the V.P. Singh-led coalition, leading to the fall of the government at the Centre. In the state, the BJP withdrew from the coalition on 26 October, reducing the Chimanbhai government to a minority. But the cunning chief minister was not one to give up easily. As V.P. Singh was replaced by Chandra Shekhar, with the Congress's support, Chimanbhai changed the alignment and the Congress came forward to support him. Many analysts view this move by the then Congress chief, Rajiv Gandhi, as the last nail on the coffin for the party in Gujarat. Chimanbhai renamed his party as Janata Dal (Secular) and later merged it with the Congress while retaining power. All the BJP could do was to cry 'betrayal of the mandate'.

Chimanbhai died on 17 February 1994 and was succeeded by Chhabildas Mehta, an old-time Congress leader who showed little signs of political ambition and probably saw himself as a mere caretaker CM. The stage was set for the March 1995 election. However, in 1995, when the assembly election was due, the BJP had successfully launched a vigorous campaign on the 'betrayal theme' and projected itself as a victim of the self-seekers of non-BJP politics. Keshubhai Patel emerged as the BJP's face for the chief ministerial post.

In the 1995 assembly election, there wasn't even an iota of doubt that the BJP had established itself as the principal player in the state. Even a cursory visit to the state would convince anyone about the BJP's victory. Given the fact that the BJP was on the margins till a decade back, its emergence from the fringe to occupy the political mainstream was not a miracle but a result of sustained work that often went unrecognized. How did this happen? How did a party, which had a very narrow base of upper caste and urban elite, transform itself into aggregating a huge mass base cutting across caste divides? Therein lies the crux of the BJP's growth, which followed a mix of conventional and unconventional methods of political aggregation.

Parshottam Rupala, a Union minister in the Modi government, used to tell an anecdote about the manner in which Modi undertook the task of the party's expansion. Rupala was inducted into the BJP in response to a call from Modi to induct *purnakalin karyakarta* (full-time volunteers) and headed the party's Amreli district unit. In those days, there was much emphasis on the practice of identifying fifty workers at each booth, to mobilize people and expand the base. Rupala introduced to the BJP many key individuals, including an influential retired bureaucrat. When Modi was in Amreli to oversee the organizational election, Rupala introduced the newcomer to him. Given his background as a bureaucrat, Modi immediately assigned him the task of making a column (called *litiganana*) in a thick register that was maintained to keep a record of the party workers across the state.

The BJP created a unique data bank of party cadres, finely categorized under different heads for the purpose of mobilization. There was a category, for instance, of party workers who were relatively affluent and owned vehicles. Those with two-wheelers were also identified. The registers were updated regularly to record any change in addresses and contact details of the foot soldiers in the party. Significantly, Modi regularly scrutinized every page of the register as long as he was the general secretary (organization) in Gujarat. There was a discernible pattern in the organization-building in Gujarat, which combined the traditional method of party-building with the non-traditional style of expansion. After the AMC elections, this methodology was experimented with and honed into a fine art in the entire state within a span of three years.

Modi kept refining his own skills as an organizer during his stint in Gujarat. What appears to have particularly helped him were two mass mobilization programmes: the Ayodhya Rath Yatra of Advani and the subsequent Ekta Yatra of Murli Manohar Joshi. In the former, Modi's role was limited to the Gujarat leg, but for the latter he was given the charge of coordination for the full route from Kanyakumari to Kashmir. In 1991, soon after the return of militancy in Jammu and Kashmir, Joshi's yatra was aimed at unfurling the Indian flag at Lal Chowk in Srinagar, the stronghold of separatists and militants. This experiment gave him exposure as an organizer at the national level, and educated him about the vulnerabilities and strengths of the party all over India.

For instance, he found a bizarre situation emerging in Karnataka, as the yatra's beginning in the state coincided with high-voltage agitation on the Cauvery water issue. Ananth Kumar, then the state BJP's general secretary and later Union minister, was assigned to oversee the yatra's arrangement in

Karnataka. As Ananth Kumar remembered, it appeared well-nigh impossible to conduct the yatra for four days in the state amid violent agitation over the river water sharing dispute with the neighbouring Tamil Nadu. 'We were quite sceptical of taking out the yatra on the planned route in the state,' he told me. Moreover, making arrangements for Joshi to address public meetings and interact with opinion-makers was even more difficult. But Modi, as the man in charge of the Ekta Yatra, was unfazed. 'He consulted all state leaders and got his own feedback from other sources, and gave us clear directions to hold the programmes as per the schedule,' recalled Kumar. 'We pulled it off quite brilliantly.'

At that time, the BJP had little presence in Karnataka, where it was seen as a party of the Hindi-speaking north. Yet, Modi managed to convince the cadre there that the party was capable of doing its job even in the most adverse circumstances. Also, the theme of the Ekta Yatra, national unity, could override linguistic preferences and strike a chord with the people of Karnataka, and Modi made good of this opportunity to present a distinctly different image of the party.

The yatra enhanced the BJP's capacity to undertake political endeavours to connect with the masses. The clinical precision in its organization was the crucial factor. In Kumar's words, Modi believed that 'God is in the details'. This became evident when the campaign reached Jammu and the government restricted its movement further. Modi made elaborate backup plans, and asked a group of senior party leaders and committed workers to stay put in Jammu while himself preparing to take along ninety-odd leaders to Srinagar. All participants were given a minute-to-minute schedule to prevent the possibility of any glitch.

And then there was another lesser-known, non-political yatra, which too revealed Modi's hidden talents. This was to

Kailash Mansarovar, in the Tibet region of China, in 1988. Keeping it purely a personal and spiritual pursuit, Modi participated in the pilgrimage, organized by the Ministry of External Affairs (MEA) under an agreement with China, keeping his political position under wraps. The MEA deputes a senior government official as liaison officer with each of the fifteen-odd batches that go for this nearly month-long pilgrimage. B.S. Baswan, the IAS officer who served as the liaison officer for Modi's batch of twenty-six pilgrims, recalls that the politician had instinctively taken up the role of the leader of the group. On 15 August, on the way to Kailash Mansarovar, the group of pilgrims celebrated Independence Day. Baswan says that Modi wore a saffron robe all through the arduous journey and pursued his spiritual quest staying detached but maintaining camaraderie with fellow pilgrims. The officer discovered Modi's background much later. Baswan, an agnostic to the core, maintains, 'He never tried to convert me to his belief. There was a humorous side of him which was quite endearing.'

His spiritual pursuit should be a personal matter, not related to politics, but I mention it here because I believe it to be intricately linked with his organizational skills. Modi has developed a particular affinity for spiritual sites all over the country. During the late '90s in Gujarat, when the BJP was still setting up its base, Modi built a rapport with leading seers and religious institutions. This is in contrast to the many previous Hindutva leaders who, as individuals, remained aloof to Hindu religion. In essence, the party's cadre network was adequately supplemented and strengthened by a parallel network of the followers of influential sects spread across the state. Here, once again, Modi's understanding of social psychology turned out to be useful. It helped the BJP project itself as a party unencumbered by a prescribed understanding of secularism and not shy of associating with Hindus and their religious symbols. In a state where communal violence had become the norm for over a decade, this approach was not only contrarian but also audacious and innovative, and it got traction among the people. It created a propitious fertile ground for the BJP in 1995, when the state was poised for the historic assembly election.

2

Electoral High | Personal Low |Exile to Delhi

Audacity in Adversity and a Splash on the National Stage

(1995–2001)

In the run-up to the 1995 assembly election, Gujarat was poised to enter its most critical political phase. The tallest leader of the influential Patel community, Chimanbhai Patel, had died a year before. His successor, Chhabildas Mehta, showed no inclination to stick to power. After Advani's arrest in Bihar, when the BJP pulled the rug from under V.P. Singh's feet and its ministers in Gujarat resigned, Chimanbhai ended the alliance and later merged his faction of the Janata Dal with the Congress—a move seen as a betrayal of the people's mandate. The BJP successfully harped on this theme by taking out rallies and meetings across the state. A new political narrative was built in the state in which the BJP was painted as the victim of the Congress's machinations. The BJP's senior-most leader, Keshubhai Patel, emerged as the tallest leader in the state.

In his role as the party general secretary (organization), Modi was working on various fronts. He was weaving the political narrative and facilitating its circulation through the cadre by organizing programmes all around the state. From 1987 to 1995, Modi, through the party's growing organizational network, had mapped the entire state with minute details of demography and placed trained BJP cadres to act in sync with the party's guidelines. The feedback system was such that anyone falling foul of the guidelines could be identified immediately.

Much of this efficiency was the direct result of meticulous record-keeping of the workers' curriculum vitae, which mentioned not only their addresses and phone numbers but also referred to their strengths and weaknesses. Though it was

29

humanly impossible for Modi to keep tabs on every worker and monitor his work, he created an organizational structure backed by technology to ensure that a given task got completed in conformity with the party's guidelines. Modi also held regular training sessions to orient the cadre to a new political culture which was at variance with the traditionalists in the BJP.

Compared with the past, what was strikingly different in the BJP's cadre composition now was the inclusion of a large number of OBCs, Dalits and tribals. Earlier, the party's cadre comprised mostly upper castes and people from urban areas. Now the party had expanded its social influence by giving adequate representation to each social group—with the apparent exclusion of religious minorities. Perhaps this exclusion was as much a result of the pro-Hindu perception of the BJP among the minorities as inhibition within the BJP to reach out to them.

The confidence with which the BJP emerged as the natural claimant of the role of 'the party for good governance' was guided more by strategic reasons than circumstances. In fact, it had shed the historical baggage that had been limiting its organic growth. The BJP's perception as a party of upper castes was diluted to a considerable extent. With the Congress ceding ground and leaving a vacuum, Modi realized it very early that the space could be easily filled by the BJP. Hence, he meticulously planned a strategy that promised to give an alternative, efficient and honest culture of governance, should the BJP come to power. Given the history of conventional political culture of the Congress—which was accused of promoting mafia and gangsters like Lateef, and of indulging in corruption—along with insecurities arising out of communal riots, the strategy found traction among people across caste lines.

People of the state started trusting the BJP. And it did not happen overnight; the process was gradual. Once again, the consistency with which committed activists of the RSS and the BJS/BJP worked across different sections of society helped them gain confidence. The relief and rescue operation after the Machchhu dam disaster in 1979 in Morbi had established the RSS's credentials in social service. In 1986–87, when Modi transitioned into the BJP, he tried to find a political equivalence of that trust by helping the party win the Ahmedabad election and developing the AMC as a model of ideal governance. People had found the governance of the AMC distinctly different from what it had been in the past; it was now aimed at improving the quality of life in the city. In effect, the transformation of the AMC's model of governance not only won people's hearts but also confirmed the BJP's bona fides for the role of 'the party for good governance' at the state level.

At the same time, the party played the victim card quite brilliantly following Chimanbhai's perceived betrayal. As the election campaign picked up, the BJP displayed a far greater astuteness than its rivals in innovating election campaign methods and taking up issues that struck a chord with the voters. One such innovative strategy was related to the deployment of party workers in strategic places like tea stalls and paan shops, and on buses and trains. Groups of party workers fanned out incognito and spoke with strangers about the invincibility of the BJP, to send across the definite message that it was in a strong position. The strategy worked as, close to election day, the BJP's victory had become a foregone conclusion.

The perception of the BJP as a strong party in Gujarat could also be attributed to a series of events which caused deep fissures in society. The KHAM theory, as an invincible social coalition for the Congress, triggered serious unrest along caste and communal lines. It appeared to be a divisive tactic to create further rift in Hindu society. This fear was confirmed when riots shook Ahmedabad in the mid-'80s for months on end, giving rise to the speculation that the Congress was bent on dividing the Hindus for political power.

It was in this phase of complete political drift that Modi built a cadre base which was highly trained and motivated. At the same time, he did not hesitate to co-opt eminent personalities and celebrities from different walks of life and align them to the BJP's political goal—to bring about a change in the culture of governance. Keshubhai Patel emerged as the most popular personality, though the Congress still had leaders like Madhavsinh Solanki and Amarsinh Chaudhary. Solanki was out of the race, as he vowed to relinquish politics following a controversy over his role in influencing the Bofors probe in his capacity as minister of state for external affairs in the P.V. Narasimha Rao government. Chaudhary did not have the stature and requisite charm to mobilize party workers and capture the people's imagination.

Thus, the stage was set for a comfortable victory for the BJP, as the Congress literally caved in and proved to be no match in the face of the former's aggressively creative campaign. For the first time, the BJP occupied the top role against the Congress and, in effect, filled the vacuum created by the departure of centralist–socialist parties like the Janata Party and Janata Dal. This was indeed an interesting development in the state's politics. Over the years, the BJP had been piggybacking on the socialist groups that formed the real axis against the Congress. Given the Sangh Parivar's limited growth in the state—on account of the perception that it was an upper-caste formation—this new development was nothing less than a tectonic political shift in the state.

In the election held in March 1995, the BJP secured 121 seats, leaving the Congress way behind at forty-five. This was certainly not the first defeat for the Congress, but it was definitive: it has not been able to return to power in Gandhinagar since that momentous day. The BJP, on the other hand, has won every assembly election since then (though between two elections it did lose power once; more on that later). Keshubhai was the obvious choice for the top post: the veteran had long years of experience in the government—he was the irrigation minister in the Janata Party government during 1977–80 and deputy chief minister in 1990. His image of a down-to-earth, elderly leader, with a background in farming, did not hurt either.

Being a Patel was an asset, as the community, humiliated most by Solanki's KHAM experiment, saw political power as a matter of honour—something Chimanbhai, too, had built on. Patels, a crucial upper caste, had contributed to the rise of the BJP, and the party was only happy to return the gesture: five of the twelve cabinet ministers at the oath-taking were Patels. (In contrast, Solanki's cabinet in 1980 did not have a single Patel, and the one in 1985 had only one.)

The BJP's victory in 1995 in the Gujarat assembly election was a cause for celebration at the national level. The party had won assembly elections in several large states by then, but defeating the Congress in what used to be its stronghold, and getting acceptance in this economically front-ranking state was a necessary value addition for its national ambitions. Since Advani's Rath Yatra began from the Somnath temple in Gujarat, the victory was also seen as the electorate's approbation of the BJP's Hindutva stratagem. On the other hand, there was all-round praise for Modi's innovative organizational expansion and tactics that had brought the entire organizational machinery in sync with the electorate's mood.

But success brings with it envy. This was what happened with Modi, whose organizational methods were frowned upon by a section of the old-timers. Shankersinh Vaghela, a redoubtable Kshatriya leader who was popular among the party cadre, grew suspicious of Modi's rising popularity. At the same time, Modi's proximity with Keshubhai and his insistence to align the government's work with the party's objective was seen as an existential threat to Vaghela. Within six months, dissension within the party's rank snowballed into a revolt. And Vaghela led this rebellion.

In the early '80s, when the BJP, as a new party, was trying to find its feet, the Sangh Parivar in Gujarat had high hopes from these two relatively young leaders, and in due time they were deputed to the BJP. Vaghela was named the BJP state president, and Modi was made the general secretary (organization). Old-timers talk of how the duo, Modi riding pillion on Vaghela's motorcycle, used to visit far-flung places in the interiors of Gujarat to expand the Sangh's activities. Though Keshubhai Patel was the most senior among them, having served as a minister in the Janata Party government, Vaghela was the face of the new party for the younger generation of urban middle-class voters—the BJP's first support base in Gujarat. Modi, meanwhile, worked behind the scenes, silently building the organization rather than his own career. Vaghela contested the 1989 Lok Sabha election from the Gandhinagar constituency and won with a margin of 2.86 lakh votes. (He vacated this seat for Advani in 1991, moving to Godhra.)

When all signs indicated that the BJP was coming to power with full majority, Patel was the obvious choice for the post of chief minister, but Vaghela nurtured his ambitions to grab the chair. As the general secretary (organization), Modi clearly backed the experienced veteran, much to the chagrin of his comrade. Vaghela should have read the signs when the party had announced that it would stick to the one-man-one-post principle, debarring him as he was an MP. But he had other plans. Even after Patel started his term in March 1995, Vaghela kept demanding the perks of power, and wanted plum positions in the cabinet and in the state-run corporations and boards for his supporters. For a cadre-based party known for its discipline, this was unusual for the BJP. Vaghela's impatience blew over in September, when Patel and some of his cabinet colleagues were visiting the US to secure funds from NRIs for the Gokul Gram scheme of rural development.

The rebellion—an unprecedented act in the party—came out in a vicious way, as Vaghela staked his claim to the top post, and some of the ministers accompanying Patel sent their fax messages in his support. Vaghela informed the assembly speaker about the formation of his breakaway faction, the Mahagujarat Janata Party, headed by his colleague Dilip Parikh. In keeping with the anti-defection law, the speaker refused to grant it the status of a separate party, as it did not have one-third of the BJP's strength. Vaghela wanted to prove his point by securing the support of enough MLAs. Thus, on Gandhi Jayanti, the whole nation was witness to this mockery being made of democracy as Vaghela virtually hijacked his supporter MLAs to Khajuraho, in the Congress-ruled Madhya Pradesh, by a chartered flight.

The central leadership found this alarming, but its response was surprising. Vajpayee rushed to Gandhinagar, held parleys with all factions and came up with a compromise formula, which was to create more trouble than solve any. No disciplinary action was taken against Vaghela; Patel was removed as chief minister; Suresh Mehta, as a leader acceptable to all factions, was installed as the new chief minister; Kashiram Rana was removed as state unit president—and finally, in a weird call, Modi was exiled from his home state. The committed workers of the party found this so shocking that they shouted slogans against Vajpayee.

The central leaders had treated with extra respect the man who hankered after power, whereas the man who selflessly worked for the party without seeking publicity was sent out into the wilderness. Vaghela was even given the ticket to contest the Lok Sabha election of May 1996. Any doubts about his worth were set to rest in this contest, as he lost from Godhra to the Congress.

He should have lost face too, but that was not the case. He continued his Gandhinagar campaign, leaving little room for Mehta to deliver governance. Not even a year had passed since the 'compromise' when, in August, Vaghela went for an ugly show of strength. He held a rally in Ahmedabad, in which his supporters arrived displaying swords on the streets. The BJP leadership finally woke up and expelled him from the party. This prompted his supporters in the assembly to demand separate sitting arrangements for the 'Mahagujarat Janata Party' (later called the Rashtriya Janata Party), and amid high drama the deputy speaker granted it. The Mehta government went for a vote of confidence, and won it 92–0, but the governor questioned the outcome. The fast-moving drama ended with the United Front government of H.D. Deve Gowda imposing President's rule in Gujarat on 19 September 1996.

Vaghela continued to explore ways to grab power and found an ally in the opposition. He became the chief minister on 23 October 1996, with the support of the Congress. The new chief minister had to get elected to the assembly, and he set his sights on Radhanpur in north Gujarat, touching Kachchh. The choice was dictated by the fact that the BJP had never won from this constituency, dominated by SCs and OBCs, and Vaghela was mistakenly perceived as an OBC leader by many.

The by-election of 5 April 1997 was a showdown like none else, and the BJP turned to the only man it could turn to in a make-or-break contest. Modi was urged to chip in, and he did. The nondescript town of Radhanpur was turned into a battleground. The BJP, RSS and their affiliate Vishwa Hindu Parishad (VHP) deployed a large number of volunteers—

estimates range from 25,000 to above 1,00,000—to canvass among some 1,49,000 voters. Vaghela, with control of the state apparatus, more than matched the numbers. Polling was marred by violence, as Vaghela resorted to every dirty trick in the book and then some. The BJP complained of blatant misuse of the police and bureaucracy, but Vaghela had his day, and he won.

But he could enjoy power for barely a year, as the Congress party chief, Sitaram Kesri, was not happy with his ways, and he was replaced by Dilip Parikh. Since Vaghela's strategy was solely aimed at power and was bereft of any desire to serve the people, the number game was bound to be short-lived. Parikh, an industrialist with no nose for power, recommended dissolution of the assembly three months later, bringing down the curtain on an unseemly drama. With people's sympathy intact, if not increased, the BJP returned to power in 1998, and Keshubhai enjoyed new-found popularity.

The irony was that Vaghela—a veteran politician with many endearing qualities who had been trained in the RSS but was driven by his hunger for power—had ended up in the Congress. As Modi was facing his first electoral test in 2002, Vaghela must have found it difficult to give his own spin to 'secularism' as the state Congress president. He remains the only leader who broke the BJP in two and formed a party of his own; others, including Uma Bharti and Kalyan Singh, were short-term aberrations who hastened to return to the fold.

Vaghela and his infamous Khajuraho–Radhanpur adventures find space here to highlight a big setback in Modi's mission in the '90s to consolidate the organization-building efforts of the '80s. There can also be no better contrast than Vaghela to understand Modi's arduous journey to power and organization (re)building.

Modi, ousted from Gujarat in 1996, did not cry foul and remained devoted to the party and the ideology. He arrived in

Delhi, to make a fresh start, without even an iota of bitterness at the injustice. It was not that Delhi was new to him. In his role as an RSS pracharak and later as BJP's state unit general secretary (organization), Modi was fairly acquainted with the national capital. But that acquaintance was not enough to give him a toehold in national politics. From Gujarat, he was straightaway inducted within the party organization as a secretary by the then BJP president, Advani. He was given charge of Haryana and Himachal Pradesh at first. In Delhi, he lived out of a room at the official residence of his colleague Dilip Sanghani, who was then the Lok Sabha member from Amreli, Gujarat. At this MP bungalow on Harishchandra Lane, Modi continued with his spartan lifestyle. In exile, with few friends and well-wishers in the party, he began his journey to a new but not so propitious terrain: Haryana and Himachal Pradesh. His background, as someone literally ousted from Gujarat, was to make this assignment even more difficult.

Haryana

His job in Haryana was certainly challenging for various reasons. The state apparently did not have much of a support base for the Sangh Parivar. Carved out of Punjab in 1966, Haryana is essentially dominated by Hindus, with a small population of Muslims concentrated in pockets like Mewat. The state is divided more along caste lines rather than religion, with Jats being the dominant caste group. Historically, the state was a bastion of the Congress, which often faced challenges from Jat-led coalitions of socialist forces. The top politician in the state was Chaudhary Devi Lal, once the deputy prime minister to V.P. Singh. He belonged to the kind of anti-Congress forces earlier represented by Chaudhary Charan Singh. Bansi Lal was another prominent face who also belonged to the Jat caste.

Given the caste equations, Haryana seemed impregnable for the BJP, which was usually identified with the upper castes, particularly Brahmins. Interestingly, people of Haryana had turned to the Arya Samaj, a movement which had originated in Gujarat. It was founded by the eighteenth-century Gujarati saint Dayanand Saraswati, whose zeal for reforming Hinduism has no parallel in recent times. Jats in the region had become followers of the Arya Samaj in large numbers, eschewing rituals that characterize traditional Hinduism. The Sangh Parivar's identification with traditional Hinduism was thus a major handicap. Modi realized it quite early in his sojourn in Haryana that he had to break new ground with audacious experimentation.

BJP workers at the district levels recall plenty of stories of how Modi insisted on having a permanent party office in every district, and wanted the offices to be equipped with computers and other modern communication gadgets. Modi also encouraged the cadre to get skilled in using computers, to fill in data about the organizational structure. This was the beginning of cadre-building in the state on the same pattern that he had successfully attempted in Gujarat. Workers were identified by their strengths in order to deploy them at short notice to realize their full potential. The idea behind all these efforts was to bring the entire organizational machinery in sync without delay.

But the most difficult task was to expand the BJP's influence in the assembly election of May 1996. Since the party alone would not be able to make a mark in the state's politics, he found it convenient to align with Bansi Lal, a notorious Sanjay Gandhi acolyte known for his excesses during the Emergency. Bansi Lal had parted company with the Congress and floated his own regional outfit, the Haryana Vikas Party (HVP), which was to merge back into the Congress in 2004. Given the party's own track record of fighting against the Emergency, there was a certain degree of discomfort within the party leadership when it came to making Bansi Lal an ally. Electoral compulsions, however, forced it to consider the matter pragmatically, as it was bound to be consigned to the margins without an alliance.

The HVP and BJP contested the election together, with the former contesting sixty-five seats, leaving the latter with twenty-five. While the HVP won thirty-three seats, the BJP won eleven, and Bansi Lal, who had served as chief minister in the '60s and '70s, returned to the post. Though the BJP was part of the government, the alliance was not destined to last long, given their differences. Modi, meanwhile, undertook a massive restructuring of the organization and roped in representatives from all social sections. Ratan Lal Kataria, a Dalit, was made the state unit president, much to the annoyance of the traditional upper-caste leadership. That was only the beginning. Modi focused particularly on women in the state in a tactical manner, to win over this section. He could sense the deep-seated prejudice against women in the male-dominated state and found it convenient to appeal to their political aspirations. At a training camp in Rohtak, he coined the slogan '*Matrutva hi netrutva*'—linking the qualities and skills of motherhood with those of leadership.

The manner in which he started projecting the BJP as a pro-women party in the state was quite instructive. In the 1999 Lok Sabha election, Modi made it a point to promote women as candidates. He asked the BJP's state unit leadership to look for women who could win elections. Though senior leaders were not happy with the move, some suggested the name of Sudha Yadav, the widow of Sukhbir Singh Yadav, a deputy commandant of the Border Security Force who had been killed in the Kargil war just a few months before. Manohar Lal Khattar (who became the chief minister in 2014) and other leaders were sent to find out if she had an inclination to contest the election. They initially found her resistant to the idea. But after two or three visits and a great deal of persuasion, Sudha Yadav agreed to contest the polls from Mahendragadh (now part of the Gurugram constituency) and went on to win. A simple housewife was turned into a leader, and she has built a successful political career since.

Modi knew it well that Sudha Yadav's candidature alone would not deliver the right social message. He organized a function in Gurgaon (now Gurugram) to mobilize funds for the election campaign of a war widow. The first contribution was made by Modi himself, and he said his mother had sent him the money from her meagre savings. He then urged others to follow suit. Within an hour, a significant amount, of Rs 7.5 lakh, was collected for Sudha Yadav's campaign. The whole event acquired emotional overtones when another Kargil martyr widow hugged Sudha and both cried holding each other. This symbolism had a far-reaching effect on voters. Given the fact that the state sends a sizeable chunk of youth to the Indian Army, Sudha Yadav's nomination as a candidate was a recognition of the state's militaristic tradition. At the same time, the event was intended to dispel any stigma attached to widowhood, which is often not looked at kindly by the traditionalists in society.

There is no doubt that Modi effected a radical change in the party's organizational structure in Haryana. The cadre network was expanded, with people from different social groups joining the party as full-time or part-time workers. After the alliance with Bansi Lal fell apart, Modi worked towards building a new alliance with Om Prakash Chautala. Since Haryana is adjacent to Delhi, the state was prone to interference from the central leadership. Modi found it difficult to overcome this handicap, even though his expansion of the party's cadre and modernization of the party offices across the state helped build a solid foundation for the future.

Himachal Pradesh

Himachal Pradesh was a different kind of challenge for Modi to grapple with. Ever since the days of the BJS, the state had always been a fertile ground for the Sangh Parivar. The state had given the BJS what was virtually its first state government, headed by Shanta Kumar, after the Emergency. Though the party fought under the banner of the Janata Party, the Shanta Kumar government was dominated by members of the BJS from 1977 till the time the ruling coalition broke up due to the Janata Parivar's internal differences. In 1990, when the BJP won the assembly election, Shanta Kumar was again chosen as chief minister. He was, however, sacked on 15 December 1992, along with the BJP governments in Uttar Pradesh, Rajasthan and Madhya Pradesh, after the demolition of the Babri mosque in Ayodhya on 6 December.

As the BJP and its forerunner, the BJS, had deep roots in the state, the challenge before Modi was quite complicated. The party's organizational structure was archaic and in disarray despite the party's formidable support base in the state. This was amply reflected when the BJP lost the assembly election in 1993 to the Congress, though the party was expected to garner sympathy after the sacking of the popularly elected government.

Modi arrived on the scene when the party's cadre was quite dejected and divided into camps of powerful satraps who were keen to protect their respective turfs. Right from the district headquarters of Mandi and Dharamshala to the state capital Shimla, Modi travelled incessantly and carried with him computers as gifts. He also instructed local leaders to purchase land for building party offices in every district. Till then they had been running the offices in an ad-hoc manner, admit many local workers who had interacted with him during that period. Those who worked with the party then acknowledge that they had never participated in any training session before Modi took charge of the state and made training a regular feature. 'We were quite often called for a day-long meeting in which senior leaders gave long lectures. It used to be one-way communication,' they recall. Instead, Modi introduced two-day training sessions, for which workers were to stay at the same place. Modi, too, would stay at the same place and interact with them over breakfast, lunch and dinner. For ordinary workers, it was a great opportunity to interact with the top leadership of the party and establish a two-way communication.

His initiative of inducting new workers from various social groups and efforts to institutionalize the party functioning was frowned upon. But that did not change his priorities. Modi enthused party workers by keeping them engaged in various programmes planned for them around the year. The constant mobilization of the party cadres across the state galvanized the party machinery and substantially shifted the party's politics from conventional thinking to a new paradigm.

Modi's fondness for the Himalayas also motivated him to consolidate his party's base in Himachal Pradesh, which he often refers to as his second home. He spent considerable time travelling across the state and climbing up the hills to familiarize himself with the state's social and political nuances. After building a robust organizational infrastructure by connecting district party offices to the state headquarters, he diverted his attention towards remoulding the party's work culture. He realized early on in his stay that leaders of stature were more interested in maintaining status quo than bringing in change. He faced resistance from the old guard at every step.

Modi devised a new strategy to build local leadership from the new generation of party leaders by holding training sessions all across the state, even at smaller places. These sessions would often last two days, with special focus on how to strengthen the organizational network and rope in social groups which were traditionally not associated with the BJP or the Sangh Parivar. For instance, legislators were asked to identify powerful organizations like the state government employees union or traders union, and to interact with them and learn about their problems at first hand. At the same time, they were told to visit different districts and ask people about their grievances. These visits were announced in advance through newspapers to enable people to come in large numbers. Legislators were told to spend the entire day with people at their place of stay, circuit houses or guest houses, and listen to complaints and raise them in the assembly.

The upshot of this exercise was remarkable. A group of legislators who were usually confined to their constituencies were effectively groomed as state-level leaders. The subsequent emergence of Prem Kumar Dhumal as a regional leader in his own right (and later a chief minister) should be seen against this background. It paved the way for the party's transition from an old leadership to a new leadership in the state. The BJP president at the time of writing, J.P. Nadda, was then a small party worker, and he belongs to the same ranks of new leadership that Modi had assiduously cultivated during the '90s. But there is no doubt that the journey for political consolidation through organization-building was quite arduous and challenging.

Modi's organization-building exercise has always been guided more by pragmatism than conventions, as was borne out by his unique stratagems in the aftermath of the 1998 assembly election in Hiamchal Pradesh. Voting was held in sixty-five of the sixty-eight constituencies, barring three reserved for STs in remote areas. A BJP candidate died before the results were announced (though he had won), necessitating a repoll. Out of the sixty-four seats the Congress won thirty-one, and a BJP rebel contesting as an independent supported it. The BJP, on the other hand, had only twenty-nine seats, reduced to twenty-eight after the death of that winning candidate. Virbhadra Singh of the Congress was invited to form the government. But Modi had still not given up. His unprecedented move was to persuade a Congress MLA, Gulab Singh Thakur, to contest the election for the post of the speaker—against the Congress's official candidate. And, surprisingly, he won, reducing the effective Congress tally by one. Virbhadra Singh was left with no option but to resign, and the governor preferred to recommend keeping the assembly under suspended animation till the results of the four pending seats were announced. (Coincidentally, less than a week later, on 19 March, Vajpayee became the prime minister.)

When the pending results came in, all the four seats went to the BJP, taking its tally to thirty-two. Moreover, the rebel MLA also returned to support the party. Still, to ensure the stability of the government headed by Prem Kumar Dhumal, who was sworn in on 24 March, Modi went ahead and co-opted Sukh Ram, a former Union minister who had quit the Congress to float his own outfit, the Himachal Vikas Congress. Facing corruption charges, he was seen as persona non grata by all— but not for a pragmatist Modi. The BJP's national leadership frowned upon the move, but Modi convinced them that Sukh Ram, with his influence over a sizeable percentage of Brahmin votes around Mandi town, was a prize catch. Moreover, Sukh Ram could only bring the numbers without any position to dictate terms to the government.

Call it his political acumen or unconventional tactics, Modi's timely moves saved the day for the BJP, and the Dhumal government went on to complete the full term. Perhaps the whole episode convinced party workers in the state that a robust and efficient organizational structure was more essential than the presence of charismatic individual leaders to sail through in assembly elections.

Himachal Pradesh proved to be a unique experiment that substantially enriched Modi in his experience as an organizational man in the BJP at the national level. In his stint as the central leader in charge of the party in Himachal Pradesh, he carried out many experiments in order to identify the strengths and weaknesses of the party. He constituted a group of twenty-odd people who were not office-bearers of the party and tasked them to trace the party's journey and its possible future. This group met in Chintpurni village of Una district and discussed threadbare the strategies to be adopted to strengthen the party. But the core strategy remained the same— that the party's apparatus would keep in touch with village-level workers who, in turn, would get the right feedback from the ground. In essence, the party's organizational structure had to be rooted to the ground. The meticulous planning in building the organizational network in Himachal Pradesh helped the party consolidate its position. That was why the BJP's vote share in the four Lok Sabha seats in Himachal Pradesh was in the range of 66–72 per cent when it secured an unprecedented mandate in 2019.

Himachal Pradesh was indeed a precursor to similar organizational experiments adopted later in Madhya Pradesh.

Madhya Pradesh

Like Himachal Pradesh, Madhya Pradesh has the history of being a strong bastion of the Sangh Parivar. In 1967, Govind Narayan Singh split the Congress and joined the Sanyukta Vidhayak Dal (SVD) of which the BJS was the biggest constituent. The BJS had acquired the position of a principled opposition against the Congress. Though the experiment did not last long, the BJS occupied the opposition space in the state effectively. But unlike in Himachal Pradesh, where it relied upon charismatic individual leadership for electoral victory, in Madhya Pradesh the BJS had in its ranks—besides charismatic leaders like Atal Bihari Vajpayee—a gifted organization man in Kushabhau Thakre. Considered to be endowed with unparalleled organizational skills, Thakre was justifiably credited for having built a disciplined party cadre from scratch. He had travelled the state so much that he was believed to have visited almost every village of the state. Thakre's thesis of party-building was quite traditional and extremely efficient.

Madhya Pradesh had emerged as a strong bastion of the Sangh Parivar even when the Congress, helmed by Jawaharlal Nehru, reigned supreme across the country. In the 1950s, the BJS won the first mayoral election in Jabalpur. This was seen as the first sign of the BJS's acceptance in the country's politics. In 1967, when the Congress's hegemony was challenged in many states following the emergence of regional satraps, Madhya Pradesh saw the emergence of the BJS as the single largest opposition, with Kailash Joshi as the leader of opposition. With the advent of the SVD, the Congress was effectively pipped to the post in the state assembly. The BJS continued to grow in strength by roping in leaders like Vijaya Raje Scindia, popularly known as the Rajmata of Gwalior, and her son, Madhavrao Scindia. The young scion of the erstwhile royal family soon parted ways and joined the Congress led by Indira Gandhi. (His son, Jyotiraditya Scindia quit the Congress and joined the BJP in 2020, bringing the story full circle.)

Those were tough times for Madhya Pradesh politics as the Congress, for the first time, suffered a vertical split in its ranks leading to the formation of the SVD government. A new pastime of toppling the government by engineering defections grew out of this uncertain political situation. And some of the past masters of this game, like Dwarka Prasad Mishra and Yashpal Kapoor, both close to Indira Gandhi, further improved their skills and used them to topple governments in many states. In those difficult times, Thakre was credited for not only keeping the BJS's flock together but also for expanding the organization exponentially.

Interestingly, along with the exponential expansion of the BJS, Madhya Pradesh emerged as a strong experimental ground for the RSS. Thakre, himself a pracharak of the RSS loaned to the BJS, found it easy to rope in RSS swayamsevaks (volunteers) for party work. He raised a strong force of the party's cadre who were rooted and trained in the RSS values. At the same time, he also mobilized sympathizers among common people through his visits to various parts of the state. He thus developed the unique 'Sangathanist' model— building a party's organizational structure on the foundation of an army of committed cadre. As a result, the BJS built a formidable base in the country's biggest state (in geographical terms back then) that was not inferior to that of the Congress, which continued to enjoy hegemony till 1977. After the Emergency, the BJS merged with the Janata Party and contested the state assembly elections. The Janata Party got an overwhelming mandate, and Kailash Joshi of the former BJS was chosen as the chief minister. During 1977–80, Joshi was replaced by Virendra Kumar Saklecha, who was again replaced by Sunderlal Patwa—both from the erstwhile BJS. Patwa remained the chief minister for less than a month, and then a resurgent Indira Gandhi dismissed the government.

When leaders owing allegiance to the BJS severed their ties with the Janata Party and formed their own party, the BJP, the new entity found itself on a strong turf in Madhya Pradesh, thanks to the presence of senior leaders, including three former chief ministers—Joshi, Saklecha and Patwa—and a host of other prominent faces. In March 1990, the BJP won the assembly election and chose Patwa once again as the chief minister. His government, however, was sacked along with the BJP governments of Uttar Pradesh and Himachal Pradesh after the demolition of the Babri mosque. After a year of President's rule, Madhya Pradesh went to polls in 1993. Surprisingly, the BJP could not win people's sympathy and lost. Digvijaya Singh of the Congress became the chief minister. A powerful regional leader, Singh went on to consolidate his position by launching a slew of social welfare measures.

It was in this context that Modi was given charge of Madhya Pradesh, with the 1998 assembly election round the corner. Having learnt his lessons in Gujarat, Haryana and Himachal in organization-building and politics, the new task was indeed challenging for him. Modi, in his role as the BJP general secretary, took up this challenge in right earnest by making cautious moves. His first and foremost task was to convince a battery of senior leadership that the conventional method of doing politics would be replaced by innovative ways of expanding the organization. He held a series of training sessions in the state to mobilize the cadre with a purpose. His emphasis on training for cadre was so intense and focused that he soon acquired the nickname of 'headmaster' among the state party veterans.

Modi's innovative ways to prepare the party cadre for the election were driven by the singular message of 'fighting to win'. He introduced new units in the party: cells in charge of information technology (IT), media and civil aviation (the last being in charge of managing travel logistics of leaders during the campaign). These cells acted in tandem to give an edge to the party's campaign. This was followed by a comprehensive roadmap on 'how to win the election'. He motivated the cadre to launch simultaneous campaigns in twenty-five-odd places to raise the pitch of the campaign and take adversaries by surprise. He also educated workers on how to spread the message of good work done by the party. 'Don't panic, fight without fear' was his advice for the party workers, who were suitably motivated and prepared for the election campaign.

At the same time, Modi carried out a detailed study of the strengths and weaknesses within the organization. He identified the areas where the party had still not reached out to voters. In Madhya Pradesh, Modi realized that politics was mainly a contesting ground between upper-caste leaders from the Congress and the BJP. There was scope for expansion among specific social groups—not only the SCs and OBCs, but also STs—especially in large tribal-dominated areas of what was to become Chhattisgarh. Co-opting these vulnerable and marginalized social sections into the BJP's fold was like plucking low-hanging fruit.

Modi mobilized the party cadre in large numbers to concentrate on the areas dominated by scheduled castes and scheduled tribes. As for tribals, particularly in Chhattisgarh, the RSS had developed a strong base through the network of the Vanvasi Kalyan Ashrams (VKAs), and the BJP's political mobilization was seamlessly aligned with the RSS's social work. This tag-along strategy was also necessitated by the paucity of funds—in 1998 the BJP was not as rich in political donations as it is now.

Along with organizational expansion and reorienting it to new priorities, Modi was conscious of populist methods that could attract voters to the BJP. He helped coin two slogans, '*Ek vote mein do pradesh* (In one vote, you will get two states)' and 'Chhattisgarh, *aage barh* (Chhattisgarh, move forward)'. These catchy slogans were intended to capture people's imagination in Chhattisgarh, which was struggling for an identity of its own. At the national level, the Vajpayee-led government had promised the creation of three new states, including Chhattisgarh. The Congress and its chief minister, Digvijaya Singh, had also promised to carve Chhattisgarh out of MP as a separate state after the polls. Yet Modi's slogans carried more conviction, as the BJP was in power in Delhi too.

Given the presence of veterans like Joshi, Saklecha, Patwa and Vikram Varma, and the larger-than-life shadow of Thakre looming over the state's organizational structure, Modi's task of persuading the leadership to fall in line and get in sync with the organizational objectives was becoming increasingly difficult. At times he found his efforts running into the wall of conventional leadership symbolized by all the stalwarts. Of course, he was in constant touch with Thakre—the national president of the party from 1998 to 2000—to learn about the distinct features of the party's organizational structure and travelled across the state to familiarize himself more with people. In negotiating the resistance from traditionalists within the BJP, he found support from yet another powerful general secretary, Pramod Mahajan. Perhaps Mahajan, whose unconventional style of functioning raised many an eyebrow within the BJP, was conscious of the resistance one had to face while ushering in change.

While the BJP was pulled in different directions at many places, the Congress, led by Digvijaya Singh, put up a coherent face. Digvijaya Singh had launched many social welfare schemes at the village and block levels to co-opt the rural political leadership by distributing doles. In terms of development, Madhya Pradesh lagged far behind many states. It had a woeful situation in the power sector, and bad roads impeded accessibility to interior villages and towns. Yet Digvijaya Singh managed to consolidate his position. The Congress won 172 of the 320 seats, leaving the BJP at 119. For the BJP, the loss, however, laid a strong foundation of organization-building in the state. It was for the first time that the party had gained ground in the tribal region and bagged a substantial number of seats reserved for the SCs and STs. Also, the whole exercise created a formidable election war machine in the state, which was to come in handy in 2003 when the party not only won the assembly election but also turned the state into an impregnable bastion where it ruled for three terms—till 2018, when the BJP lost narrowly to the Congress despite a higher vote share. (In 2020, however, with several Congress MLAs moving to the BJP, the party came back to power in the state.)

As a result of Modi's exemplary devotion to the cause of the party, he was meanwhile appreciated and promoted to the post of the national general secretary (organization) on 19 May 1998. This post was so crucial that it had been held by only three stalwarts earlier: Deendayal Upadhyaya, Sunder Singh Bhandari and Kushabhai Thakre. Also, Modi was then named the spokesperson of the party—which was now in power at the national level. That was where he was before his grand return to the home state.

3

The Orator | The Reformer | The Administrator

Gujarat in Full Grasp, Delhi within Sight

(2001–14)

Three days before he finally settled in his office as the chief minister of Gujarat, Narendra Modi asked his staff to arrange some bare necessities—a clean room with an attached bathroom in the Gandhinagar Circuit House, a flat bed and two landline phones. Incessant travels in cars across the country had caused him a perennial back problem, so the bed had to be flat. After nearly six years of exile from his home state, Modi's return as its chief political executive in 2001 was set in an interesting context.

The politics of the state had undergone a radical change in Modi's absence. Chief Minister Keshubhai Patel, who had headed the BJP's first government in the state in 1995, was showing signs of ageing and losing his touch. Charges of nepotism and inefficient administration were common. The law-and-order situation was weakening and so was Keshubhai's grip on power—so much so that, during a heated discussion in a cabinet meeting, a minister accused him of lying (and resigned immediately).

After a split and several changes of the government, a tired BJP was divided into various factions, each pulling the party in a different direction. It was losing people's trust, and in the September–October 2000 elections to local bodies, the party was routed across the state. The results shocked not only the BJP leadership but also, apparently, the winner, the Congress, as well as the media. The BJP lost power in five of the state's six municipal corporations, including in Rajkot, where it had been invincible since 1982—the party's first victory in the state.

The BJP lost power in each of the nineteen district panchayats, whereas in 1995 it had won eighteen of them, with the seats coming down from 82 per cent to 27 per cent. For taluka panchayats, the seat percentage fell from 67 to 33. The alarm bells were ringing ahead of the assembly polls due in 2002.

What proved to be Keshubhai's undoing were the reports of abject mismanagement in the wake of the massive earthquake that rocked Gujarat, with its epicentre in the Kachchh district, on 26 January 2001. Leading cities and towns of Kachchh, as well as the neighbouring Saurashtra region, were razed to the ground. Effects were felt even in Ahmedabad, where several buildings came down like a pack of cards—a school here, a high-rise apartment block there. The total casualties were estimated to be slightly above 20,000, though unofficial estimates put the toll far higher.

The extent of devastation was so enormous and unprecedented that even offices of all the government facilities, including camps of the army and the Border Security Force (BSF)—Kachchh shares a border with Pakistan—were destroyed to a large extent. The relief operations initially faced handicaps on several fronts.

Modi rushed from Delhi to Bhuj and initiated measures to meet the situation. Given his own experience in organizing relief operations after the Machchhu dam break tragedy of 1979, Modi should have been the obvious choice for leading the operations in the state. But Keshubhai chose to cold-shoulder him instead. Even the central leadership—primarily Prime Minister Vajpayee and Home Minister Advani—avoided pushing his case to lead relief efforts. Advani, who represented the Gandhinagar Lok Sabha constituency, was hesitant to restore Modi's role in Gujarat politics despite his position as the BJP general secretary. The reason was obvious. Keshubhai had turned against Modi. A section of senior state leaders, like the former chief minister Suresh Mehta and Union ministers Kashiram Rana and Harin Pathak, also feared that his presence would ultimately eclipse them. These veterans had developed considerable stakes in maintaining status quo.

Yet, in the aftermath of the earthquake, with reports of shoddy relief and rehabilitation works, the central leadership, particularly Vajpayee and Advani, became increasingly conscious of the fact that under Keshubhai's leadership it was highly unlikely that the party would retain power in this crucial state. After months of prevarication, the top duo finally made up their collective mind to effect a change. They held a day-long meeting in the Delhi office, consulted almost every state leader who mattered and finally announced the replacement that surprised many, even if it seemed obvious very soon.

Patel tendered his resignation on 3 October 2001, and Modi arrived in Gandhinagar two days later—to the welcome of some of the old colleagues and party workers. He greeted each of the mediapersons by name, even asking health updates from some, showing he was never out of touch with his home state despite his exile. In his first remarks to the media, he compared his task ahead as a One Day International game of cricket, fast-paced and result-oriented, as opposed to laidback Test cricket.

He was sworn in as chief minister on 7 October. The newcomer did not want to rock the boat so soon, and the cabinet formation had no surprises. A sulking Suresh Mehta, who had thought he was the natural replacement to Keshubhai once again, was part of the cabinet, with the same portfolio, industry, as before. Among the eleven cabinet ministers and twenty-seven ministers of state, the Patel factor was conspicuous—as the BJP did not want to send out a wrong signal to the influential community in shunting out Keshubhai. Nitin Patel (who later served as deputy chief minister from August 2016 to September 2021) headed the all-important finance department and Anandiben Patel (later a chief minister) was the education minister.

Modi was aware of the multiple challenges he would face in this new assignment. As a man who had evolved with the organization, he knew that he would find the going tough if the BJP's organization was not aligned with the government. Since Keshubhai was yet to vacate the official residence of the chief minister, Modi chose to stay in the state guest house.

Though a quintessential organization man, Modi was practically a novice in governance. He was not even a legislator when he assumed the role of the chief minister. Similarly, the complexities of governance and the labyrinth of bureaucratese were not easy to master. Right from the beginning, he started learning the trick of 'reading files' from bureaucrats who were working closely with him.

But he soon realized that his real challenge was at the organizational level, where he was facing stiff resistance. And that challenge came to the fore when he needed to win an assembly seat as a constitutional prerequisite for his continuance as the chief minister. Modi wanted to contest from Ellisbridge, a prestigious seat in the upper-middle-class part of Ahmedabad then represented by Haren Pandya, the minister of state for home. Pandya, an RSS veteran and Keshubhai's trusted aide, declined to vacate the seat for Modi.

Being an organization man, Modi knew in his heart that the beginning was not good. He looked for another seat and found his old colleague Vajubhai Vala, an RSS–BJS veteran, more than eager to relinquish his Rajkot-2 seat in his favour. Modi won the January by-election, though he realized he would desperately need to reorient the organization that had gone wayward and align it with the government's work. He was also woefully short of time as the assembly election was due within a year.

His twin tasks, to recap, were to put in order the government and the party—and keep them on the same page, unlike in the past, when they would be at loggerheads.

Modi began by meticulously picking up the issues that needed to be addressed at the governance level. To restore confidence among people, he launched a massive rehabilitation programme in the earthquake-hit Kachchh and Saurashtra, and started rebuilding the Bhuj district headquarters from scratch. He channelized all energies of the government, the party and society to rebuild Bhuj, like the proverbial Phoenix rising from the ashes. The reconstruction of Bhuj was intended to send across a definite message of restoring people's confidence in the government.

This was a positive step as Gujarat had an indifferent record of governance. Former chief ministers, such as Madhavsinh Solanki and Amarsinh Chaudhary, were brought in for their political skills in managing community and caste contradictions, not for administrative acumen. Governance was always given short shrift, resulting in a series of communal and caste riots during the'80s. Chimanbhai Patel, in his second innings during 1989–94, had attempted to bring economic and administrative issues to the fore. With his relentless focus on the fast-tracking the Sardar Sarovar Narmada dam project, he aspired to win the tag of a development-oriented chief minister, though his first priority remained politics. Keshubhai was largely a politician of the old mould, even if his party claimed to be known for good governance. He finally had the upper hand over the party, as became evident in the tardy rehabilitation work after the earthquake.

Set against this background, the speedy reconstruction of Kachchh assumed greater significance than any usual rehabilitation activity. It was a much-needed move to restore people's confidence in the government and the party. To rebuild Kachchh and other quake-affected parts, funds were needed in large amounts, and Modi turned to the corporate sector, a step that gelled well with the entrepreneurial spirit of the state. In October 2001, the state government organized a meeting with industry leaders, 'Global Gujarat, Resurgent Gujarat'. Modi's penchant for communication was at work here: 'global' appealed to the large diaspora of Gujaratis abroad, and 'resurgent' was the call to build the state anew under a new leadership. In February 2002, yet another 'Resurgent Gujarat' conference was organized, with the help of the Gujarat Chamber of Commerce and Industry, the Federation of Indian Chambers of Commerce and Industry and the key ministries of the Union government. Industry titans pledged all help to Kachchh in particular and to the state in general, with investments in new economic activities. In turn, Modi assured them complete ease of doing business, eliminating red tape.

At the same time, Modi's no-nonsense ways started imparting a sense of accountability in the entire bureaucratic machinery, which had often appeared to be at war within. He silently observed the functioning of each institution of governance in order to comprehend the complexities of administration. Officers who worked with him closely back then testify that he is an incredibly fast learner.

Here is an episode that reveals his way of learning lessons in governance. All district collectors were to attend a conference over two days, and the new chief minister was invited as the chief guest. Modi accepted the invitation, on the condition that he would not be a participant but only an observer. Taking a seat in the back of the auditorium, he allowed the conference to go on in its own flow. He tried to understand the manner in which the district collectors and senior officers interacted with one another on the issue of governance, and how issues of even village and taluka levels were discussed and resolved.

At the end of the meeting, he issued clear instructions to all officers: 'I am a vagabond and will travel all across the state to learn administration but also to monitor progress. Please do not make elaborate arrangements for me as I will stay in the circuit house or state guest house.' Thus began his journey for learning the art of governance.

A senior official who has been working with him since the beginning points out that Modi was not averse to expressing his ignorance on any issue and seeking expert guidance. One of his innovative initiatives in governance was organizing a series of training camps for state employees along with their senior-most bosses. They all brainstormed over issues concerning people and formulated resolutions. The government was thus ready with a set of suitable government orders (GOs) at the conclusion of the training sessions.

Looking back on those training sessions, a senior bureaucrat recalls that all the servants of the people, right from minister to secretary and junior staff, were asked to board state-run buses to reach the venue—no private transport allowed, because everyone was equal. Everyone would participate in each session as an equal stakeholder. During lunch and dinner, a junior officer could offer suggestions to the secretary or the minister, and all would interact freely in an informal atmosphere, unmindful of hierarchies. The chief minister, too, would chat with everyone and ask them about their problems and their senior officials. At the end of the session, everyone would be on the same page and aligned to one agenda—to resolve the issues that had appeared intractable in the beginning. 'This was the most innovative experience as every government employee became a stakeholder in the system,' the official says.

Modi was in the midst of introducing a slew of changes in public administration when, on the morning of 27 February 2002, the train-burning tragedy happened in Godhra. As many as fifty-nine passengers, including women and children, were burnt alive in the S-6 coach of the Sabarmati Express, which was returning from Ayodhya. Volunteers of the Vishwa Hindu Parishad (VHP), known as *karsevaks*, as they had participated in a campaign demanding the construction of a Ram temple in Ayodhya, were returning to Gujarat in batches. They became the target of mob fury motivated on communal lines. The gruesome incident angered the Hindu majority, and the VHP's call for a state-wide protest shutdown the next day acted as the trigger for them to vent their anger. Cities and towns, especially Ahmedabad but also the eastern border of the state, were engulfed in violence, with Muslims bearing the brunt. Close to 2000 people died over the weeks before normality was restored.

The inadequacies of governance came to the fore when the state administration was found woefully wanting in its efforts to contain the situation. The army and the central forces were deployed to bring the situation under control. Since the remit of this book is solely concerned with the organizational skills that Modi deployed to align with the government's agenda the party's avowed political and social goals, the Godhra and post-Godhra turbulence in the state will not get a detailed study.

While what happened on that fateful morning in Godhra is well known, little attention is paid to what was happening in Gandhinagar at about the same time. In the assembly, Finance Minister Nitin Patel was presenting the annual budget of the state, the first from the Modi government and the last before the coming election. The document would serve as Modi's mission statement, and a close reading of it is necessary to understand his priorities and vision.

Since this was the first budget under his watch after the earthquake, Modi had already organized a meet of entrepreneurs called 'Resurgent Gujarat' as a precursor to 'Vibrant Gujarat'. At the meet, entrepreneurs were asked to invest in the state. They were given assurance that a propitious climate would be created for the growth of industry. Along with this thrust on the industry, the budget made provisions for an innovative idea of 'Samras Gram' (Consensus Village)—launched the previous year, on 11 October, Jayaprakash Narayan's birth anniversary. Under the scheme, the state would give financial rewards to those villages which would choose their pradhans and sarpanchs of the gram panchayat by consensus, that is, without elections. The aim was to promote harmony and avoid conflict. While elections are usually fought by parties with their symbols, the panchayat law had kept parties out of village-level elections. Modi's understanding was that this was intended to maintain the family-like spirit of village communities, and avoiding elections would promote the same spirit. In his very first attempt at introducing new models of governance, he saw the 'Samras Gram Panchayat' concept as 'governance through consensus', in which the chosen representatives would work with more enthusiasm and responsibility. The opposition was quick to term it 'murder of democracy', but Modi responded (at one of the events where financial rewards and prizes were distributed to 'samras' villages): 'When India elects its President unanimously it is called the victory of democracy, but when a village elects its entire panchayat unanimously in Gujarat the opposition finds it murder.'

The samras concept seems in consonance with the Sangh Parivar's philosophy, where consensus is the preferred mode of electing heads of any affiliated organization, be it the RSS, BJP, VHP, ABVP, the Bharatiya Mazdoor Sangh (BMS) or the Bharatiya Kisan Sangh (BKS). This approach broadly stems from the Sangh Parivar's understanding that society gets divided along caste/communal lines during elections, which leave a bitter impact.

For Modi, there was another source of inspiration, too. 'I was a small boy when I heard a noted Gandhian and aide of Vinoba Bhave, Dr Dwarka Das Joshi, when he visited my native place, Vadnagar, during the Bhoodan campaign. The thrust of his campaign was: "Don't divide the village,"' Modi once told me, explaining the genesis of samras. He thus strove determinedly to arrive at social consensus at the village level to pre-empt social fissures. On the political level, this was an astute strategy to neutralize the possibility of any adversary trying to take advantage of any social discord in villages.

With an eye on the elections, in Modi's view, the administration should not only deliver to people but must also be seen to be delivering to people. There was no virtue in remaining aloof and toiling away in Gandhinagar. He wanted his government to reach out to people. So, the budget announced a series of *melas*, or fairs, the platforms for a variety of social welfare initiatives. During the 'Lok Kalyan Mela', for example, beneficiaries were invited to receive their benefits at the fair, held across the state, in which officials would hand them over their entitlements.

Another novelty in the budget was the 'Panch Gram Mitra Yojana'. According to it, five persons would be identified in each village and would devote themselves exclusively to five key themes: *krishi* (agriculture), *shiksha* (education), *arogya* (health care), *vikas* (development) and *jankalyan* (people's welfare). This team of five people, usually youngsters, in every village had the potential of creating a parallel organizational network to promote the government's image. Among other initiatives, the state gifted bicycles to school-going girls in those areas where the literacy rate was as abysmally low as below 25 per cent. Gujarat's female literacy rate in 2002 was 57.8 per cent, and the move was a nudge to promote education. The scheme was later extended to the whole state. (By Census

2011, the female literacy rate in the state had touched 69.68 per cent.)

Having created a parallel and formidable organizational structure to enable the government's unhindered outreach to diverse social sections, particularly those that had felt neglected for years on end, Modi seamlessly aligned it with his political objective for the BJP. In essence, the BJP's organizational machinery and the state government schemes were brought perfectly in sync with each other.

Meanwhile, the spiral of violence had created political uncertainty for a short period. After five relatively uneventful months in Gandhinagar, Modi was suddenly an international newsmaker: some saw in him the true icon of Hindutva, a Hindu *hridaysamrat*, stronger than Advani and Bal Thackeray, while others started comparing him to Hitler. One could only like him or loathe him; there was no middle way, and no ignoring him. Modi, unwittingly, was inviting controversies, and some in the party doubted his ability to deliver victory with his new, larger-than-life persona. But eventually, the party decided to go to the polls under his leadership.

Uncertainty was created especially by the party leadership as it discussed the question of replacing Modi in the face of growing secular criticism. Vajpayee even dispatched Arun Jaitley to Gandhinagar to secure Modi's resignation, which was to be announced at the party's national executive meeting in April 2002. However, at that conclave in Goa, the younger generation led by Pramod Mahajan and Jaitley gave strong indications to the veterans that sacking Modi would not be in consonance with the party's ideology, and Vajpayee dropped the matter in no time.

Though the term of the assembly was till March 2003, Modi wanted to dispel all uncertainty and seek a fresh mandate of his own. On 18 July, he recommended the governor to dissolve the assembly. Elections should have been held soon after that, but the Election Commission had other views. Chief election commissioner, J.M. Lyngdoh, insisted that full normality had not been restored in the state after the communal violence, and that a large number of displaced Muslims had still been living in relief camps, often far away from their homes. He ruled out holding elections till the situation returned to normal.

A frustrated Modi then wanted to go directly to people, to '*paanch karod* Gujaratis' (5 crore Gujaratis—emphasizing that he meant all people, including the minorities). By turns unapologetic and belligerent, he now wanted to articulate his vision to the people and seek a mandate for it. He wanted to do so in a way that would also recharge the party workers' confidence—which had been down since the resounding defeat in the local body polls—and get them going after votes. His solution was to go back to his earlier days of yatras with Advani and Joshi. He would take out yatras across the state, talk directly to people to answer accusations flying in the media and, by organizing these events, also oil the rusting machinery of the party.

The 'Gujarat Gaurav Yatra', or the pride rally, was, needless to say, planned meticulously. Once a week, he would take a break from Gandhinagar and governance, and head for a district. The venue would usually have religious connotations, preferably a pilgrimage town. (The first one was Ambaji in north Gujarat, a Shakti Peeth and a very popular pilgrim town.) Invited on the dais would be a BJP leader of national stature, and party workers would ensure that people would turn up in good numbers.

A completely new Modi was emerging in these weekly outings: a fiery orator who would mesmerize the audience immediately. So far, he had been known to work silently behind the scenes. Now, he was becoming a public man. This was the start of a long phase during which he learnt to effortlessly change his public persona—and many more changes were to come, according to circumstances. The Gaurav Yatra, initially frowned upon by party veterans sitting in Delhi, started making news for the content of his speeches, but the speeches were neither the usual, old-fashioned ideological expositions nor entertaining talks mixed with poetry and rhetoric. He was building a rapport with people, boldly saying things that had never been said before and inviting the audience to join in by asking them yes–no questions, and people responded wholeheartedly.

He also equated all criticism from the opposition, media and the secular critics as criticism directed at the Gujarati people, and posed the coming election as a vote on Gujarati 'asmita'. Asmita, a term popularized by K.M. Munshi, a Congress member of the Constituent Assembly and also a highly popular novelist in Gujarati, includes shades of 'identity' and 'pride'.

The top leadership, that is, the Vajpayee–Advani duo who were then at their peak of popularity, were not altogether happy with Modi's invocation of Gujarati pride. They believed appealing to 'gaurav' would not be enough to tide over the anti-incumbency factor, especially after the rout in the local body election less than a year earlier. Modi, however, was confident of his reading of the people's mood.

By the time the election dates were announced, and the opposition made plans to launch the campaign, Modi had already completed an extensive campaign in the form of the Gaurav Yatra. In an early instance of his assertiveness and self-confidence, he sought a free hand in choosing the party candidates, surprising the central leaders. He believed this was a necessity, after the Vaghela rebellion that had split the party and led to several bouts of government change. Advani and others accepted his demand but insisted on a few names, including that of Haren Pandya. Modi would not relent. When the central leaders refused to take his no, Modi complained of chest pain and got himself admitted to the Civil Hospital, forcing them to relent.

The Gujarat assembly election rarely made national news, but this time it was international news. Modi rose to the occasion and used the opportunity to criticize the practice of secularism he had seen so far. He could have targeted the state opposition leaders—his friend-turned-foe Vaghela was the state Congress president now—but he aimed higher, targeting national opposition leaders, especially the Congress chief, Sonia Gandhi, and President of Pakistan, Pervez Musharraf.

The results were not all that surprising in hindsight: the BJP won 127 seats, ten more than in the previous assembly. The vote share went up, at 49.85 per cent (it was 42.51 per cent in 1995 and 44.81 per cent in 1998). Notably, the BJP increased its popularity among the marginalized sections: it won nine of the thirteen seats reserved for the SCs and thirteen of the twenty-six seats reserved for the STs.

For the BJP, there was an important lesson here. The party, right from the BJS days, had spoken of 'good governance'—well before the expression became a catchphrase. Its first chief minister, Shanta Kumar in Himachal Pradesh (1977–80), worked hard to improve governance. His defeat, however, had made the party doubt that voters rewarded development works. It had come to believe that good governance was bad politics. Modi's 2007 victory made the party change that view and embrace 'good governance' as electoral strategy across the country.

The cabinet had not many changes, except that Vajubhai Vala made a return as the finance minister. (Vala was to later become governor of Karnataka, but not before setting a record for the highest number of state budgets presented—eighteen.)

There were only ten ministers and six ministers of state—among the smallest cabinets in the history of the state. Well before the 91st Amendment to the Constitution restricted the size of the cabinet in 2004, this was Modi's first hint at 'Minimum Government, Maximum Governance'.

After the results began yet another tough spell for Modi. He had to fight on several fronts; the only relief was from the thoroughly decimated state Congress. Firstly, he now had the full mandate and he had to deliver on it. Secondly, he had to execute his vision of governance. Thirdly, he had to tackle the malcontents within the party, anxious to grab power.

He started afresh, with an exclusive focus on changing the image of Gujarat and—his constant refrain—the 'paanch karod Gujaratis'. Perhaps he found in this focus an antidote to the campaign built by a section of the intelligentsia that depicted him as the villain responsible for the communal violence. Modi chose not to respond to the agendas set by the media, opposition and a section of disgruntled leaders within the BJP, and drew his own grand plans for the state. He launched a slew of initiatives under the name of 'Beti Bachao' (save the girl child), to correct the skewed sex ratio and attend to the issue of growing malnutrition among children.

For the first time, the state machinery was mobilized to celebrate the birth of the girl child. In this programme, the birth of girls was celebrated in all villages to educate masses on the importance of girls in the family. The programme was aimed at gently dissuading people from the practice of going for abortion in case the foetus was found to be female. This practice has consistently caused an alarming decline in the sex ratio of the state. The initiative was supplemented by festivals on the opening day of the academic year to celebrate girls entering the school for the first time. Such fairs and fests were not just for optics: Census 2011 was to show a 13 per cent rise over 2001 in the literacy rate of girls and a 29.77 per cent decrease in the school dropout ratio.

Along with this programme was launched another scheme for reaching out to pregnant women, giving them nutritional diets and educating them about the importance of taking proper nutrition for the growth of the foetus. Most of these programmes were held as festivals in which the entire bureaucracy participated and the whole society came together as a major stakeholder.

At the same time, Modi needed to give an impression of a no-nonsense administrator. Given the history of violence in the state, which formed the immediate backdrop of the election, Modi decided to go strictly by the rulebook in containing extremist elements, irrespective of their political affiliation or religion. Hooligans who had taken to streets or caused communal strife in the name of being members of the VHP were contained effectively. The message was driven home quite clearly that they would not be spared if they decided to disturb peace. Anarchic elements within the VHP found themselves hemmed in from all sides. Thus, unlike with some other states, in Gujarat the VHP or any fringe group did not have a field day on Valentine's Day, nor were there any incidents of anyone disturbing the celebrations of minorities' festivals.

Modi then took up a major task which had been bothering him for long. Gujarat is a water-deficit state where droughts are perennial, and the chief minister turned his attention to change the landscape of Saurashtra by initiating several measures. The Sardar Sarovar dam project was the chief solution to the crisis, but since the work on it had been suspended following a Supreme Court order, farmers had gone ahead with their local solutions—building check dams and *boribunds*. The Keshubhai Patel government had decided to extend support to this initiative by launching the Sardar Patel Sahbhagi Jal Sanchay Yojana in 2000. Its implementation, however, lacked energy.

Modi injected enthusiasm, and over five years—even as the Supreme Court gave a green signal to the Narmada project—the state built more than 1 lakh check dams and boribunds, with people's participation, and farmers' groups contributed Rs 250–300 crore. According to an Indian Institute of Management Ahmedabad study, thanks to the scheme, groundwater and wells in the region were recharged, and about 20 lakh bighas of land could be protected against drought. The cost of a typical check dam was Rs 1,58,000, whereas it delivered total benefits worth Rs 2,51,582 in three years. In some villages people had to buy water supplied through tankers for ten to eleven months a year at the cost of Rs 200 to Rs 250 per month. Check dams curtailed this period by six months.

For better communication with cabinet colleagues, Modi hit upon a novel idea: since he did not have a family at home, he would often join one of the ministers, within the same neighbourhood, for dinner and discuss developments in an informal setting.

Also on the communication front, he charted a new territory: there were a few next-generation leaders who were tech-savvy, but Modi went a step further and opened new channels of communication using the Internet and social media. He was not only among the first but also the most successful of political leaders taking to Facebook and Twitter. This helped him in not only countering the allegations coming from large sections of the mainstream media but also creating a rapport with the increasing number of supporters at home and abroad. Obviously, the first benefit of the exercise was in consolidating the party organization.

Soon after the 2002 election victory, instead of turning to populism, Modi used the 'honeymoon period' to introduce several unpopular but badly needed reforms, creating a template which would be put to use again and again, also at the national level after he became prime minister. With the kind of confidence that comes only from conviction or people's support, Modi did away with conventions. One of them was to appoint MLAs who did not find a place in the cabinet and other senior party workers to the numerous boards and corporations of the state government. Modi ended the perk, as he nominated bureaucrats to these organizations, signalling that what mattered was efficiency and service to the people—and not keeping everybody happy. When every politician is addicted to announcing freebies and doles, it needs guts to stop the existing ones. One of the key factors behind the groundwater depletion in Gujarat was free and cheap power to farmers, who freely overdrew water. The Modi government decided to restrict power supply to them to only four hours. At the same time, they were asked to pay user charges for electricity. This was a clear departure from the established norms. His concerns were adequately outlined in the budget 2003–04.

In his second stint as the chief minister, he launched a pioneering move in power reforms, 'Jyoti Gram Yojana', which became a model for the rest of the country. Under this scheme, round-the-clock power supply of one-phase electricity for domestic consumption was assured to each household after the bifurcation of feeders for domestic and agricultural/industrial consumption. Since electricity for agricultural purpose is heavily subsidized, it is often used for domestic consumption. The bifurcation of feeders enabled power companies to raise the bill according to the user's actual consumption. Also, the tariffs for farmers were tripled, and in 2004, penalties were slapped on around 60,000 defaulters.

He was ready for protests—and they came from an organization closer home: the RSS-backed Bharatiya Kisan

Sangh (BKS). Those in the vanguard of the protests against the power reform mostly belonged to a section of Patels, who are large landholders. It was a battle of nerves in which Modi steadfastly declined to blink, despite incessant attacks from within the Sangh Parivar. Those who worked closely with Modi at that time say that the chief minister was extremely pained at the reluctance of agitating BKS leaders and farmers to understand the government's scheme, which would ultimately benefit only them. 'They don't realize now, but they will praise me after ten years,' one of them recalls Modi telling him.

An officer who worked with the chief minister's office back then said that Modi's conviction in regard to regulating power supply to farmers was so strong that he did not think twice before risking his political career on this. He was convinced that unless power supply was regulated, drought-prone Kachchh and Saurashtra would turn out be an ecological disaster, with excessive drawing of underground water. He refused to budge, and the agitation was wound up after a while.

Given the entrepreneurial nature of the state, trade, commerce and industry were never far from the new chief minister's mind. The communal violence had led to speculations whether the industry would continue to repose faith in the state, and Modi wanted to dispel such doubts. He had in mind an investor conference, but on a scale that would make a statement in itself. The result was the Vibrant Gujarat Global Investors Summit, held in Ahmedabad during 28–30 September 2003—to coincide with the state's popular Navaratri festival. In this gathering of top corporate leaders of India, supported by the United Nations Industrial Development Organization (UNIDO), Ratan Tata famously remarked, 'You are stupid if you are not in Gujarat.' Mukesh Ambani and Kumar Mangalam Birla, too, praised Modi's leadership and vision. Other veterans of India Inc. also endorsed this view while the state government came forward with an investment-friendly approach. In three days, industrialists signed seventy-six memorandums of understanding (MoUs), intending to invest a total of $14 billion in the state.

The event was so successful that the state decided to organize it every two years (though in January, to coincide with the kite-flying festival of Uttarayan), and later a dedicated venue was set up for it in Gandhinagar. Also, the figures of the investment intentions announced at the bi-annual events prompted state after state to launch their own editions of investor meets. Behind the tag of 'vibrant' was Modi's acumen for branding and coining keywords. While 'Vibrant Gujarat' is usually seen as an event to garner investments, the first edition was also witness to another, less-remembered achievement: as it was time for the Navratri festival (during which, incidentally, Modi keeps a fast), the state also organized garba, the local popular dance form, and at one place in Ahmedabad, the participants joined in such numbers that the circle they formed was 1.5 km long. Minorities also participated, going by reports. Thus, the event finally lifted the dark clouds of reported 'insecurities' and communal divisions, and Gujarat was finally back to routine.

When the financial year was over, Gujarat was well on its way to lead the country: its economy grew by 15.4 per cent in 2003–04, up from 10.15 per cent in 2002–03, and nearly double what it was during Keshubhai's last year, 7.75 per cent in 2001–02.

On Modi's agenda there were other matters too, apart from the economy—the social sector, for example. In 2004 he launched initiatives to co-opt marginalized sections, like the SCs and STs, on a large scale. The government sponsored the publication of Dr B.R. Ambedkar's writings in Gujarati. This was accompanied by various schemes to promote education and provide financial assistance to those living on the margins. The idea was to promote education among the SCs and STs and check dropout rates. Such an initiative was bound to raise the literacy level, which was abysmally low among these sections of society. But the most transformative idea was to encourage inter-caste marriages in the state, and the scheme was named after Ambedkar's second wife, Savita, who was a Brahmin by caste. Another scheme, to promote multiple weddings at one venue to save expenses, was launched in the name of Ambedkar's first wife, Ramabai Ambedkar. The discourse around Ambedkar was appropriated astutely in the state's actions that were targeted to win over the marginalized sections in an active manner.

All these initiatives bore fruit, as Gujarat topped the list of states in terms of reduction of poverty in 2005. The Planning Commission pegged the rate of poverty in Gujarat at 14.07 per cent, against the national average of 26.10 per cent. Poverty alleviation brought previously marginalized sections into the economic mainstream, creating a class that has always been on Modi's radar—the 'neo middle class'. The robust economic growth in the state helped create opportunities in every sphere—agriculture, manufacturing and service sectors.

The agriculture sector was given a fillip with the introduction of technology in a massive way. Slogans like 'from soil to satellite' and 'from lab to land' were coined to familiarize farmers with the use of modern gadgets and innovation to plan their crops efficiently. With this emphasis, Modi gave a call for ushering in the next 'green revolution' in a state otherwise known for water scarcity.

What emboldened the Modi government was the court's permission to raise the height of the Sardar Sarovar dam by 15 metres, which enabled the state to fill twenty-one rivers and many other water bodies using excess rainwater from the Narmada dam. The diversion of excess water from the Narmada adequately fed the parched tracts of Saurashtra and Kachchh subsequently. These efforts were complemented by the Sujalam Sufalam scheme, aimed at diverting water from the Narmada's main canal to the north Gujarat rivers.

Gujarat experienced a radical change in its agriculture sector as it got bumper yields in 2005. It was in this context that the idea of raising farmers' income substantially was mooted. In villages, the efficient distribution of power enabled the Gujarat Electricity Board to supply twenty-four-hour, three-phase electricity supply for domestic consumption. Gujarat was already among the most urbanized states, and now its rural areas were acquiring all the amenities of cities and towns. This led Modi to claim, at a meeting of the National Development Council (NDC), that Gujarat had effectively obliterated the rural–urban divide.

By the middle of 2005, Modi had successfully aligned a strong force of nearly 5 lakh state employees with his government's agenda. Modi referred to them as 'karmayogis'. These employees, ranging from the chief secretary to a class-four employee, had undergone training sessions of about twenty hours, where they learnt meditation and yoga too. At the end of the training, they took a pledge to work for the welfare of people with complete devotion. This was a master strategy, turning nearly 5 lakh state employees into stakeholders in the system. In 2004, they were asked to pursue fifty-three projects in twenty-five districts and 270 projects in 225 talukas on their own, according to the state budget of 2004–05. In essence, they had the responsibility of designing and executing these projects meant for the welfare of people. The objective of the karmayogi initiative was to sensitize the huge government machinery to people's issues and to bring it out from moribund indolence to a state of rejuvenation. This huge machinery was yet again a parallel organizational structure that got seamlessly aligned to Modi's political objectives of pursuing the development of

Gujarat and the welfare of its 5 crore people as prime tasks. Of course, the government's agenda in turn became the agenda of the BJP.

The government thus gradually modelled itself on a corporate culture that was identified with quick delivery, efficiency and transparency. Modi had been tech-savvy even earlier, and now, as chief minister, with a knack for innovating governance practices, he was bound to turn to the use of technology to ensure efficiency and transparency. During his regime, many government offices underwent a makeover and now looked like corporate workplaces. The training of state employees came in handy for them to adapt to this new work culture. For the first time, the gap between government officials and citizens was bridged successfully as the former became accountable for the success of the government's schemes. A sustained effort was made to convey the message that government machinery is integral to social life. This was quite an innovative way of reducing the gap between the government and the governed.

Meanwhile, on the political front, few were surprised with the results of the local body elections in 2003 and 2005. All the six municipal corporations were again under the BJP's belt. The party still had a lot to cover in the district and taluka panchayats in the rural side, but it still had an upper hand over the Congress.

The 2004 Lok Sabha election did surprise all. This was the first time (and the only time so far) when the party's tally actually dipped in Gujarat, and dipped by a third, as the Vajpayee government lost the polls. In Gujarat, the central leadership had given a decisive role to the disgruntled former chief ministers— Keshubhai Patel had a say in the ticket distribution, whereas Suresh Mehta (who had lost the 2002 assembly polls in spite of the BJP wave) was in charge of the campaign committee. Though Vajpayee, in his 'Manali Musings' of June 2004, was to blame the loss on Gujarat riots and Modi's continuance as chief minister, the party was actually coming around to acknowledge the mistake of not letting Modi lead the charge in the state.

Keshubhai and Company, however, continued to plot ways to dethrone Modi. There had been open rebellions in 2003 and 2004 too, with Patel, Mehta, Rana and others rushing to Delhi, complaining against Modi's 'autocratic' ways and 'unpopularity' among the party cadre. In August 2005, the rebellion reached its peak as the key rebels got a significant number of MLAs to gather at Patel's residence in Gandhinagar in a show of strength. Patel called him a dictator and even said that a 'mini emergency' was prevailing in Gujarat. As if this was not enough, in the cabinet expansion that month, Gordhan Zadafia refused to take oath, while Purshottam Solanki, a minister, demanded Modi's resignation.

Out of power, they were unhappy at Modi's rising acceptance across social groups. A confident Modi remained predictably unperturbed by the happenings right before his eyes, and kept quiet. I was then with STAR News and made a request for his interview, to get on record his views on the rebellion. I was invited to Gandhinagar, but to my dismay he preferred to talk not about his rivals but about his efforts to bring water to Saurashtra and Kachchh. In hindsight, it showed his focus on development rather than petty quarrels.

Meanwhile, a supposed setback for Modi was the denial of visa by the US government (he had been invited to Florida to address a gathering of the Asian–American Hoteliers Association, with a large number of Gujaratis among them). The George W. Bush administration cited the human-rights record of the state. (Modi then addressed the March 2005 meet via video-conferencing.) Within no time, the UK government followed suit and refused visa to him. The ensuing international debate turned Modi into a larger hero.

An unruffled Modi continued his work within the state. Presenting the 2006–07 budget himself, now that he also held the charge of the finance department, Modi outlined a development roadmap for Gujarat. What he conjured up was an ambitious dream of nothing less than placing Gujarat in the ranks of the developed nations. The time had come to project Gujarat as an international brand, distinct from the image of India. In the international context, Gujarat was seen as a destination for foreign industries where the atmosphere was conducive for business.

There, however, were several social indicators that sullied the state's image. One of them was the sex ratio: the state had only 878 girls against 1000 boys below six years of age, one of the worst figures in the country. In his budget speech, Modi said, 'A society that discriminates between man and woman is bound to be doomed.' He implored members across party lines to launch a vigorous awareness campaign against the practice of female foeticide.

In April 2006, Modi surprised all by sitting on a fast, for fifty-one hours, to protest the injustice meted out to Gujarat. The Narmada Valley Authority had granted permission to raise the height of the Sardar Sarovar dam to 100 metres. (The Supreme Court had, in the historic October 2000 judgment, permitted the construction of the dam in tranches, depending on the relief and rehabilitation of the affected people.) But the water resources minister of the UPA government, Saifuddin Soz, chose to review the decision and thus stall the move. The project, since its inception, has been an emotional issue for Gujaratis, and every chief minister has found support for it cutting across party lines. Modi, in opposing the Centre's vacillation, sat on a fast in public and forced the UPA government to fast-track the dam construction.

In 2006, yet another happy story emerged from the state. The Gujarat Electricity Board, which had been incurring chronic losses, turned around and posted a profit of Rs 49 crore for the first time. This development had a significant bearing in the whole nation as the electricity board in every state was notorious for incurring huge losses. The power reform initiative Modi had undertaken was showing positive results. The state electricity board was unbundled in seven different companies to facilitate the distribution of power efficiently. Since an assured power supply for twenty-four hours made consumers happy, user charges were collected efficiently and power theft was substantially curbed. All this turned the loss-making board into a profitable venture.

It would not be wrong to say that by the end of 2006, Gujarat had emerged as a model state for attracting investments from across the country and abroad. Modi travelled extensively and visited nine states while his colleagues in the cabinet went across other parts of the country to project Gujarat as a top investment and tourism destination. These visiting delegations invited people from the other states to come and see for themselves the development that Gujarat had ushered in. This was indeed a concerted attempt to sell the image of Gujarat as a state cut above the rest and worthy of emulation for the rest of India. This image got firmly entrenched among people across the country.

The growth story was, however, substantially eclipsed by the human development index (HDI) prepared by the United Nation Development Programme (UNDP), which showed the state's continued poor performance on various social indicators like infant mortality, nutrition, literacy and health. An emphasis was laid on ensuring overall development, particularly in the rural parts of the state, where poverty was stark and education and health-care facilities were scarce. In

2008, the state government declared its intent to 'increase the momentum of development through infrastructural facilities and simultaneously want to take a firm step ahead to put Gujarat at par with the developed countries in terms of the HDI'. This was indeed a tall order, given Gujarat's poor record in HDI. Yet it was an extraordinary declaration of intent and a good beginning for the government to take up the cause of improving the HDI.

This was one of the periods of robust growth in the agriculture sector, which galloped at a 12 per cent growth rate. The government organized a series of Krishi Mahotsava, or agriculture festivals, across the state to educate farmers about new methods of farming that utilized technology. In areas facing water scarcity, farmers were encouraged to use the dripping and sprinkle methods of irrigation to get 'more crop per drop'. Close coordination with Israel on this irrigation technology enabled farmers with large landholding to enhance their yields substantially.

Another major boost to agriculture came through Modi's scheme of Jal Shakti, which rejuvenated the villages of north Gujarat, Saurashtra, Kachchh and the eastern belt by bringing water from the Mahi and Narmada rivers into lakes, check dams and dried rivers. The result was an increase in grass availability that in turn raised the milk yield, according to the budget 2008–09.

Yet, around the same time, a lobby of farmers backed by the opposition and a section of BKS leaders started protests against the government's promotion of industrialization. Since the Gujarat government was quite active in promoting special economic zones (SEZs), the allegation was that reckless industrialization had deprived farmers of their agricultural land. Contrary to the perception, however, the state's coverage under agricultural land had actually increased substantially.

Thus, when the assembly election of 2007 was around the corner, Modi found himself, as usual, battling on several fronts, mostly from within his party, and a demotivated Congress in opposition was the only solace. Keshubhai, who had not contested in 2002 and had preferred the Rajya Sabha membership, went to the extent of blessing the Congress after giving a call for change—all this while being within the BJP. A section of the party MLAs was also unhappy with Modi's leadership. As Modi went for fresh faces, those left out went to the opposition—and the Congress happily gave the ticket to many of them, including some who were facing charges of having participated in the 2002 violence.

As the election campaign started, it was clear that Modi's relationship with the voters was intact. At rally after rally, he exhorted people to vote for 'kamal' (the lotus, the party symbol) for the single reason: 'vikas', development. The Congress, on the other hand, harped on the communal divisions, and its president, Sonia Gandhi, finally dropped a bombshell when she referred to the Modi government as *'maut ke saudagar'*, the merchants of death. Her reference was to the police encounter killing of Sohrabuddin Sheikh, a notorious criminal. Having resisted the divisive discourse so far, Modi was left with no choice but to respond. At every rally, he would ask the audience if Sohrabuddin was a terrorist or not, and people would loudly reply in the affirmative. Modi's oratory was complemented by his linguistic skills (he is a published poet): he termed the Congress-led government in the Centre as the 'Delhi sultanate' and Sonia, with all due respect, as 'begum', encapsulating a long history in keywords that an average voter could relate to.

There are reasons to believe that Modi wanted to put the past behind and seek mandate only on his record of development, yet the opposition changed the game, polarized the scene and gifted the election to him. The result, largely predictable after Sonia Gandhi's blunder, was the BJP's victory, with 117 seats. Again, Modi continued to expand the social base of the party, making it acceptable within new groups. The party won eleven of the thirteen SC seats and the same number of ST seats out of the twenty-six.

Two consecutive victories had now proven Modi's higher stature, and commentators started talking of him as potential prime minister material. In response, Modi gave two signals: firstly, in his victory speech at the party office he urged the cadre and people to help him prepare grand celebrations for 'Swarnim' (Golden) Gujarat on the occasion of the fiftieth anniversary of the state's foundation, coming up on 1 May 2010. This was his way of saying he was content to serve the state for the next five years. The second thing he did revealed an unusual, emotional side of the otherwise aloof man. At a meeting of the party's winners in the assembly, Modi broke down. He said he never was and never intended to become larger than the party, which he compared with the figure of mother—and then he sought a glass of water mid-sentence and sobbed. This image of a victor showing such humility was to repeat in 2014 too.

That year, he put his cabinet colleague Parshottam Rupala in charge of the state unit of the party, and that was the end of a long history of rebellions. By the time the Lok Sabha election was held in 2009, Modi had diligently ironed out innumerable creases. The BJP had become the party of first choice for Gujaratis, and the win of fifteen seats out of twenty-six, despite the loss at the national level, was credited to Modi. The defeat of Vaghela, a minister in the outgoing UPA-1 government, was the icing on the cake.

With the 2010 celebrations in mind, Modi again devoted himself to his job. Having created the infrastructure and attended to the chronic shortcomings that came in the way of development, Modi started projecting the image of 'Golden Gujarat' to give a further fillip to people's expectations and aspirations. To make Gujarat a finance hub, like London and Singapore, he mooted the concept of creating a new city near Gandhinagar and named it Gujarat International Financial Tec-City (GIFT). To make it a functional finance hub, however, amendments were needed in the relevant laws, and that was where the UPA government at the Centre was less than cooperative. Still, GIFT took off as an international finance hub, and nearly all leading financial firms and markets have opened offices in this ultra-modern complex that serves as a template for the Central government's Smart City initiative of 2014.

The incremental changes in Gujarat helped transform how it was perceived—from a state of trade and commerce to a highly industrialized state. The manner in which Modi later attracted Tata Motors' Nano car project from West Bengal to Gujarat set an example for proactive policies to win over the industry. Till 2010 Gujarat had got permission to set up nearly 60 SEZs to facilitate the industry to grow. At the same time, the government decided to create special investment regions (SIRs) to consolidate gains of massive industrialization. The state continued to attract massive investments, the size of many small states' full budgets: it secured MoUs worth Rs 12 lakh crore at the Vibrant Gujarat Global Investors' Summit of 2009, in which 600 representatives from forty-six nations participated.

What was particularly unique in this approach was Modi's awareness of the environmental impact of industrialization and the growing international concerns about ecological balance. The state laid emphasis on alternative sources of energy, especially solar and wind, and planted 935 sq. km of mangroves and enhanced green cover to claim carbon credits.

The impression that robust and rapid industrialization would damage the environment was neutralized by this approach. Gujarat's progress on solar energy has won international accolades.

As Gujarat boasts the longest coastline in the country, ports were developed to facilitate transportation through sea routes for the entire country—a move projected with the tagline 'development of Gujarat is development of India'. This narrative gradually began permeating people's perception.

In fact, 2011–12 was the year of a conscious and deliberate projection of Gujarat as a role model for the rest of India. Commentators started talking about a 'Gujarat model' of development, and it evoked curiosity all across the country. Modi and his ministers sold this unique model by travelling the length and breadth of the country, and arguing that this approach rested on all-round development by promoting service, manufacturing and agriculture in equal measure. 'Rather than developing one sector at the cost of the other, our principle has been holistic development at a steady pace,' noted Finance Minister Vajubhai Vala in his budget speech of 2011–12.

What was this model? In an interview with me in 2011, Modi expounded on the topic, 'If I were to explain it, I would say that I would not let a "single-pillar" growth model to develop in the state. The Gujarat model is based on three pillars: industry, services and agriculture. You will get balanced development only if you focus equally on each sector. In the Gujarat model, we go the extra mile to take care of micromanagement.'

The holistic development ensured that there was no contest in the assembly election of 2012. It was becoming a rather monotonous convention—the same rebels (Patel had quit the BJP and launched his own outfit, the Gujarat Parivartan Party), the same talk of why and how Modi was bound to be defeated, and the same result eventually. By now, the BJP's famed election-winning machine was in place, with Amit Shah, Modi's former minister of state for home, firmly in charge. By now, Modi had trained the party cadre to be in fighting spirits. Now aided by Shah and Rupala, Modi knew key workers in every constituency and filled them with enthusiasm to work at the booth level in such a way as to not miss out a single voter.

The result: the BJP won 115 seats, with 47.85 per cent vote share. The Parivartan Party, which had been hotly talked about, had only two winners, one of them being Patel himself. (He would merge the outfit into the BJP in 2014.) This victory made Modi the tallest leader in the party, which was yet to come out of the shock of the Lok Sabha 2009 defeat under Advani's leadership. While there were a few three-term chief ministers in the BJP and elsewhere, none of them was being talked about, with fond hopes, in far-flung places across India. As soon as the Gujarat results were announced, the talk turned to 2014. Unlike his first reactions to the 2007 verdict, Modi this time chose to speak in Hindi instead of Gujarati—indicating that he was now addressing the whole country. The signal was loud and clear.

But the national plans would have to wait, as he again devoted himself to serve Gujarat first. Among new achievements, symbolizing the emergence of a new Gujarat, an international convention hall came up in Gandhinagar in two years flat. It was to host the biannual Vibrant Gujarat summit as well as similar events. Named Mahatma Mandir, the convention hall has all facilities on a par with international standards and ranks above the Vigyan Bhavan of New Delhi. The most modern convention centre in the name of Mahatma Gandhi evoked a wide range of responses, from approbation to opprobrium. The opulence and five-star facilities were considered at odds with

Gandhian values. However, the scale of grandness was regarded as yet another sign of Gujarat's economic prowess.

Modi then turned to another great son of Gujarat, Sardar Vallabhbhai Patel. He decided to pay an unusual tribute to the Iron Man of India by building a tall statue, taller than the tallest, just like the leader himself. Announcing the proposal at a press conference in October 2013, the chief minister said the statue would come up on the island of Sadhubet near the Sardar Sarovar Dam on the Narmada. It was a project to commemorate the contribution of Sardar Patel in uniting the nation by persuading hundreds of principalities to merge with India. Therefore, the proposed statue was named the Statue of Unity. Modi's appeal and vision were no longer limited to the state, and Patel too was a leader of the whole India. So an appeal was made to all citizens of the country to donate a token of their agricultural tools for the making of the statue. All these efforts were just precursors to Modi's arrival on the national scene in an unprecedented way.

The nationwide mobilization of people and political leaders for this project enabled Modi to cement his numero-uno position after this third successive victory in the assembly elections. The party's grassroots workers were engaged in the mobilization of people in villages to donate agricultural implements. Senior BJP leaders and social activists from all over the country attended the foundation-laying ceremony of the statue on Sardar Patel's birth anniversary, 31 October 2013.

Towards the fag end of Modi's chief ministership, Gujarat's economy had continued to grow well above 10 per cent for over a decade, and a new slogan was coined to indicate the state's inclusive growth: '*Sauno saath, sauno vikas* (Cooperation of all, development of all)'. In effect, people's participation was sought at the social level to give development the thrust of a mass movement. When Modi became the prime ministerial candidate of the BJP in 2014, with the logic of continuity, the Hindi translation of the Gujarati slogan became a national catchphrase, '*Sabka saath, sabka vikas*'.

4

The Hiccup | The Pickup | The Knockout

Richter 282: A Quake That Changed India's Political Landscape

(2013–14)

The BJP's national executive meeting in Goa in 2013 was one of the most transformative events in the political life of the country. On 7 June, the sky was overcast with the onset of the monsoon. The flights to Goa largely carried either members of the BJP's national executive or mediapersons. As usual in the monsoon season, the landing of the planes was not smooth. But the tremors that were felt by the party delegates after the landing were far more disturbing than the minor jerks in the air.

The delegates were informed about the fact that a sulking L.K. Advani had chosen to stay away from the meeting. The reason was obvious. The Goa national executive was almost set to declare Narendra Modi as the numero uno in the party by projecting him as chairman of the campaign committee. Advani seemed to oppose the idea of declaring anyone as the leader of the BJP. For the first time in his long innings as a political activist, Advani chose to stay away from the national executive meeting of the BJP or its forebear, the Bharatiya Jana Sangh (BJS). Advani's absence was quite palpable at this critical moment.

Advani was not alone in having reservations about the party's move to project Modi as chairman of the party's campaign committee for the 2014 Lok Sabha election. Yashwant Sinha, Shatrughan Sinha and Uma Bharti, too, stayed away from the national executive meeting on one pretext or another. There was a discernible fault line in the top BJP leadership on the eve of the Lok Sabha battle. What complicated the issue was stiff resistance by the Janata Dal (United), an important constituent of the National Democratic Alliance (NDA), to the projection of Modi as the future leader. JD(U) leader Nitish Kumar had threatened to part ways with the BJP if it went ahead with Modi as the leader.

This was the background against which the Goa national executive meet was held in 2013. Since the issue was too sensitive and involved a leader who was credited to have built the party from scratch, the party leadership handled the crisis with the utmost maturity and deftness. Just as the meeting began, the BJP spokespersons were adequately briefed to explain away Advani's absence by citing 'health reasons'. BJP president Rajnath Singh emphasized many times that Advani's ill health prevented him from attending the event. 'His blessings are always with us,' Singh claimed while addressing and welcoming the delegates on 8 June. Though a plane was kept waiting at the Delhi airport for Advani to fly to Goa, if he were to change his mind in the nick of time, Advani remained obstinate. He was sitting at his Delhi home in perfectly fine health. This fact was known to all senior leaders but was kept a closely guarded secret.

But Advani's absence was not easy to ignore, given his stature in the party. A section of senior leaders was of the opinion to shelve the decision to declare Modi as the campaign committee chairman, which in effect meant naming the prime ministerial candidate for the Lok Sabha polls. But the writing on the wall was clear. A large majority of delegates overwhelmingly favoured the decision and wanted to clinch the issue at the executive meet. But should they go ahead in the absence of the patriarchal figure? RSS point person Suresh Soni, who was present at the executive meet, prodded the leadership to take the decision even in the absence of Advani. Rajnath Singh concurred with this view, and Modi was declared as the party's numero uno on 9 June. That Modi was chosen to be the party's prime ministerial candidate became evident when, at a meeting of workers, Rajnath Singh chose to speak before Modi, in acknowledgement of the latter's greater popularity and acceptance as leader.

Overwhelmed by the gesture, Modi spoke at length about the history of the BJP and referred to the sacrifices made by party workers in Goa for its liberation in the 1960s. In his speech, he made a distinction between *padabhar* (weight of a post) and *karyabhar* (weight of duties). Perhaps aware of the circumstances under which he was taking over, Modi invoked the strength of the party's discipline and organizational strength and recalled the contribution of BJS leader Jagannath Rao Joshi, who had led the movement for the liberation of Goa from Portuguese rule. The seamless manner in which the Goa national executive meet was conducted marked the beginning of a new era in the BJP. It was a clear transition of leadership, from the older generation of the Atal–Advani era to the younger leadership comprising Modi, Rajnath Singh and Arun Jaitley.

But that transition was not smooth and faced hurdles a day after the executive meet concluded. On 10 June, Advani resigned from three crucial party fora—the national executive, the parliamentary board and the election committee—raising serious doubts about the manner in which the party leadership had been conducting its affairs. In a letter to the BJP president, Rajnath Singh, he said, 'For some time, I have been finding it difficult to reconcile either with the current functioning of the party, or the direction in which it is going.'* There is no doubt that Advani's resignation was a big blow to the efforts of reorienting the party to a new leadership. Given Advani's stature and the timing of his resignation, the mood at the Goa national executive meet was devoid of exuberance and had a touch of

---

* 'Full Text of L K Advani's Resignation Letter to Rajnath Singh', *Indian Express*, 10 June 2013, https://indianexpress.com/article/india/latest-news/full-text-of-l-k-advanis-resignation-letter-to-rajnath-singh/

sadness to it. Here it would be pertinent to dwell at some
length on the significance of Advani in the BJP's organizational
structure. Among BJP workers, Advani always came across as a
father figure who had built the BJP during its years of struggle.
And he was essentially known as an organization man.

Advani, along with Vajpayee, dominated the party for over
four decades like a colossus. Both the leaders were given free rein
in running the party as they wished. Till 2004, when the BJP lost
the election, they were unquestionable leaders. Advani became
the leader of opposition in the Lok Sabha while Vajpayee receded
to the background. But after the electoral setback, in a dramatic
turn of events, on 18 October 2004 the then BJP president M.
Venkaiah Naidu resigned citing 'personal reasons'. Advani took
over as the party president while retaining his position as leader
of opposition. Of course, Advani's holding on to two significant
posts did not go well with the RSS and other constituents of the
Sangh Parivar. It was seen as unilateralism of the worst order in
the party. In fact, there is a history behind the RSS's suspicion
of the growing culture of unilateralism under the leadership of
Advani. There were instances, like when Vajpayee had been
declared as the BJP's prime ministerial candidate ahead of the
1996 Lok Sabha election, when Advani made a decision on his
own without wider consultation. The RSS had been nursing a
grudge against him on this issue. His decision to capture both
the important posts—party president as well as the leader of
opposition in the Lok Sabha—was seen as consistent with the
streak of unilateralism he had shown in the past while taking
decisions on party matters.

In fact, after the 2004 Lok Sabha defeat, Advani did not
realize that he had lost considerable clout within the Sangh
Parivar. A powerful section of the RSS–VHP–BMS leadership
was ranged against him. What appeared to make his position
vulnerable was his trip to Pakistan, where he quoted Sarojini

Naidu to describe Mohammad Ali Jinnah as 'secular'. Perhaps Advani's intellectual formulation was guided by his companion on the tour, Sudheendra Kulkarni, though the latter denied it. Whatever may be the reason, Advani's indiscretion touched a raw nerve in the Sangh Parivar and within the BJP. On his return from Karachi to India, Advani was practically cornered. He resigned from the BJP president's post. It was at this point that Modi rushed in from Gandhinagar and persuaded all leaders of the Sangh Parivar, and ultimately prevailed upon them to let Advani take the final call. Advani later withdrew his resignation and continued till the end of 2005. He was replaced by Rajnath Singh. Since then, his relations with the RSS and its other constituents have run into a rough phase. Subsequent to this, he launched a yatra along with Rajnath Singh to mobilize the party's cadre but could not get the kind of traction as he was expecting. The yatra was cut short early because of the death of a key party strategist and close confidant, Pramod Mahajan, in a fratricidal feud. Though Advani was projected in 2009 as the BJP's prime ministerial candidate, he could not capture the imagination of the electorate. The BJP's humiliating drubbing in the elections proved conclusively that Advani's leadership was now subject to the law of diminishing returns. A significant section of the Sangh Parivar realized the limitations associated with Advani.

He, however, was not one to let go of his ambitions so quickly. For the first time he was seen to be out of sync with the mood of the party's cadre, yet he pushed ahead by launching yet another yatra on 11 October 2011 from Sitabdiara, the birthplace of Jayaprakash Narayan in Bihar, in the presence of Chief Minister Nitish Kumar. This yatra was planned when the Congress-led UPA government was facing allegations of corruption. Advani tried to connect with people by taking up the issue of corruption and black money. The yatra started very well as Nitish Kumar flagged it off. But the backdrop against which the yatra was held did not sit well with Sangh Parivar leaders. Initially, Advani wanted to begin his yatra from Gujarat, to which Modi readily agreed. However, Modi suggested that instead of travelling by road, Advani, given his age, should consider the option of criss-crossing the country on a chopper. Later, Advani chose Bihar and invited Nitish Kumar, knowing full well that there was a history of animosity between Modi and Kumar. Still, the BJP leadership threw its full weight behind Advani's yatra, which evoked a degree of response. But there was a perceptible loss of charm in Advani's personality as compared to his past experiences of leading the chariot to Ayodhya and on various other issues. Obviously, with the 2014 Lok Sabha election on the horizon, Advani was consistently trying to retain his top position in the party. His resistance to Modi's elevation as the leader of the campaign came at this juncture, when he was being seen as doggedly pursuing his personal ambitions at the expense of the organization. Evidently, Advani's political conduct was not consistent with the training of a swayamsevak of the Sangh. Yet his political stature was such that the Sangh Parivar leadership considered it wise to keep such 'human failings' under wraps.

The Goa national executive meet set the tone for the future of the BJP. At the public meeting after the executive meet, Modi's projection as the future prime ministerial candidate became a foregone conclusion, though it was left ambiguous deliberately— not that there were any doubts about it, but so that the decision would evolve through due process. On 14 September 2013, the BJP's parliamentary board meeting was called at the party's Ashoka Road headquarters to decide whether Modi should be named the BJP's official prime ministerial candidate. Once again, Advani tried to create a roadblock. He seemed to have got influenced by the advice that he should stay away from the meeting. Of course, his absence got many tongues wagging, but it did not have any impact on the process of decision-making. Modi was declared the party's prime ministerial candidate for the Lok Sabha election. Interestingly, Modi personally visited Advani after the decision was announced to pay obeisance to the elderly leader. The whole episode significantly undermined Advani's position but clearly put a seal on Modi's stature as the undisputed number-one leader in the party. And that set the stage for the Lok Sabha election.

Right from the word go, Modi was conscious of the organizational strengths and limitations of the BJP. Perhaps he was the only leader after Advani who could claim to have visited every district headquarters in the country during his stint as an RSS pracharak and subsequently as a BJP leader. As Gujarat chief minister, his name was familiar to people in most parts of the country. Yet, he had just risen to the national scene, and now, in a short time, some kind of magic had to be woven around him, for him to be able to appeal to people across the country. Given the impression of Manmohan Singh as a weak prime minister, who was less of a leader than a follower of Congress president Sonia Gandhi, Modi was projected as a strong and decisive leader who had delivered good governance in Gujarat. The general impression among people was that given a chance Modi would deliver the same at the national stage. Of course, Modi's name began exuding optimism and hope. And Modi started articulating that optimism in his speeches. A catchy slogan was coined as the campaign theme: '*Achche din aanewale hain* (Good times are coming)'.

Nobody could anticipate the intensity of people's desire for change and for a strong leadership. The 'Gujarat model' was a readymade example that measured up to their aspirations. In the Lok Sabha election, the party's organizational structure had to be aligned with the campaign theme in order to project Modi as an answer to people's yearning for change. And this time, the BJP strategists did not repeat the mistakes of 2009, when the prime ministerial candidate Advani had attacked Manmohan Singh by calling him 'the weakest prime minister of India ever'. Obviously, Modi knew it better than most that a negative campaign against the rivals was bad strategy. So the campaign was woven around the persona of Modi, which was not cast in the image of conventional politicians.

But a campaign based on a 'personality cult' has its limitations too. It needs to be backed by organizational strength. Modi had already learnt his lessons from the 2004 Lok Sabha election, when a powerful campaign around the BJP's most charismatic leader, Atal Bihari Vajpayee, could not yield results. In sharp contrast, a mild-mannered political lightweight like Manmohan Singh, backed by Sonia Gandhi, was catapulted to the centre stage and became the prime minister—not for one but two terms. Here was a lesson: that it would be a wrong strategy to bank solely on charisma and ignore organizational backup.

Since 2001, when he became the Gujarat chief minister, Modi had assiduously cultivated his image as a leader exclusively devoted to his state. He had consciously avoided projecting any national role for himself. In the meantime, the party leadership at the organizational level had undergone many changes, which had no connection with Modi. In essence, he was irrelevant to the organizational structure at the national level, though he was the most powerful leader in Gujarat.

However, a decade of Congress rule (2004–14) under Manmohan Singh had put not only the BJP's organizational structure under stress but also threatened the RSS and its affiliated organizations. Ever since the UPA came to power, there had been consistent attempts to pin down Modi on multiple cases, ranging from the communal riots of 2002 to the killings of criminals in encounters with the state police. The

UPA government brazenly deployed legal and not-so-legal arsenal to corner the Modi government.

In a deposition before the Special Investigation Team (SIT), constituted by the Supreme Court, Modi was subjected to an inquisition that lasted several hours at the CBI office in Gandhinagar in March 2010.* He was questioned particularly in connection with a case of communal violence in which Ehsan Jafri, a former MP from Congress, had been killed. Modi was eventually given a clean chit by the SIT. In one of the encounter cases, the killing of Sohrabuddin Sheikh, Gujarat's minister of state for home, Amit Shah, had to not only resign but was also jailed by the investigative agency, the CBI, apparently at the insistence of the Centre. Though the CBI could not produce evidence of his involvement in the killing, through his incarceration the UPA strategists were trying to mount pressure on Shah to manufacture false evidence against Modi in order to stymie the latter's rising popularity across India. Since Shah steadfastly stood his ground, the strategy did not work.

As if this was not enough, an attempt was made to create a revolt-like situation in the state bureaucracy by creating dissension. A small band of bureaucrats raised a banner of revolt against the government in order to put Modi in the dock. Along with these tactical manoeuvres, the UPA government unleashed a flurry of investigations into terror cases and linked them with the RSS, its affiliates and some Hindu organizations.

---

* 'SIT Completes Modi Interrogation', *The Hindu*, 28 March 2010, https://www.thehindu.com/news/national/other-states//article60600370.ece; 'Gujarat Riots: Modi Questioned by SIT for over Five Hours', *Times of India*, 27 March 2010, https://timesofindia.indiatimes.com/india/gujaratriots-modi-questioned-by-sit-for-over-five-hours/articleshow/5730708.cms; also see SIT chief R.K. Raghavan's comments later in his memoir, *A Road Well Travelled*, Westland, 2020, https://www.hindustantimes.com/india-news/pm-modi-didn-t-accept-tea-during-9-hour-questioning-by-gujarat-riots-sit-probe-chief/story-Cc61UEAiStF47GikrCRkeK.html

For instance, the Malegaon blasts of 2006 were linked to an unknown organization called Abhinav Bharat, which drew its strength either from the Sangh Parivar's organizations or some religious bodies having close association with the RSS. This was clearly intended to curb the growth of the RSS by branding it as a terrorist organization. An important functionary of the RSS, Indresh Kumar, was referred to as the man behind planning and organizing terror acts.

The UPA was emboldened by the two terms it earned at the Centre, as the opposition, mainly the BJP, was totally adrift and lacklustre to pose any formidable challenge. The only concern they genuinely had was the possibility of Modi emerging as the rallying point for the burgeoning new middle class and younger generations which had become impatient with insipid governance and growing corruption. These impatient and vocal sections appeared to be attracted towards the idea of a strong leader who could stand in sharp contrast to the then prime minister, whose image of being subservient to the Nehru–Gandhi family was all too prevalent. The prestige of the office of the prime minister touched an all-time low when Rahul Gandhi, only an MP, tore an ordinance passed by the cabinet in September 2013. Hours before Manmohan Singh was to meet the visiting US President Barack Obama, Rahul told a press conference that the ordinance to shield convicted legislators was 'nonsense' in his personal opinion.

As Manmohan Singh's second term drew to a close, Modi emerged as a serious challenge to the UPA in popular perception. The UPA had launched a witch-hunt against the RSS and its affiliates on the issue of so-called Hindutva terror and tried to pin down Modi on the pretext of criminal cases, but that had eventually prompted factions within the Sangh Parivar to close ranks and put up a united fight on behalf of Modi. Interestingly, every move of the UPA aimed at wearing down Modi had instead substantially consolidated his position within the BJP. Curiously, there were many in the UPA, and even within the BJP and its allies, who could not see the writing on the wall.

Rajnath Singh, as the BJP's national president, was quick to discern the political mood. He completely threw in his lot with Modi and unreservedly endorsed him as the prime ministerial candidate. The skilled and great organizer that he is, Modi quickly got up to the task of crafting the campaign. In Gujarat, he had developed a powerful parallel network that used to work as a force multiplier for the BJP's organizational campaign. With Modi on the centre stage, the BJP's own organization network, along with the cadres of associated organizations, completely aligned with the strong network of the RSS and its affiliates across the country. The overseas organizations of the RSS and the BJP also chipped in to launch a well-organized and concerted campaign that projected Modi as the man who symbolized people's intense desire for change.

If one goes by the conventional understanding of politics, the BJP's organizational strength did not have the capacity to mobilize voters across the country to win a clear majority. It was an unachievable target by any stretch of the imagination. In the 2009 Lok Sabha election, the BJP had performed quite dismally and won only 116 seats. The party found its base shrunken in large states like Uttar Pradesh, where its tally was abysmally low at ten out of the eighty. In terms of vote share, the BJP hovered around 18.80 per cent—the lowest since the BJP came into political reckoning in the 1991 general election, following the Ram Janmabhoomi agitation. Of course, there were apparent signs of contraction within the party's organizational set-up. Having faced a hostile government for a decade, the cadre were despondent.

Modi's projection as the prime ministerial candidate galvanized a demoralized cadre of the BJP, RSS and affiliates. More than that, Modi's charisma mesmerized voters who were utterly impatient with the '*chalta hai*' (business as usual) approach that characterized the attitude of a rigidly status-quoist bureaucracy over the years. There was high expectation in the air as people believed that Modi would radically transform the way the country was governed. His credentials were well established as the Gujarat chief minister who had carried out development work with single-minded devotion, irrespective of the opprobrium heaped on him for being communally prejudiced. Instead of getting intimidated, Modi resolutely followed his own path and endeared himself to the masses by consistently defying the conventional politics of the time.

In one academic discussion, the phenomenon of his emergence was seen in close comparison with the ascendancy of Margret Thatcher in Britain, where obstructive socialism and aggressive trade unionism had become the defining characteristics of social and political lives, and considerably irked the people. Thatcher's aggressive push for free market and determined will to stand up against unionism appealed to people and helped her build the image of an 'iron lady' of Britain. Thatcherism was the zeitgeist of the '80s and '90s. Though there may appear certain features similar in their rise, it will be oversimplification to draw any conclusions from the two dissimilar epochs and personalities.

There is no doubt that Modi's emergence was substantially propelled by the cardinal mistake of the Congress to foist a prime minister whose demeanour was more bureaucratic than what would befit the country's top political executive. The smugness of the Nehru–Gandhi family was further enhanced by the fact that the UPA won the second term with a bigger mandate in 2009. This victory had set in complacency in the Congress leadership, which grossly misread the people's mood, marked by a subterranean anger welling up over the arrogance and indolence that defined the behaviour of the ruling party, giving rise to rampant corruption. In such a setting, Modi's carefully crafted image of a decisive and hard-working politician who neither indulges nor tolerates corruption found instant acceptance among the electorate. His slogan, '*Na khaunga, na khane doonga* (Neither do I take cuts, nor will allow others to take cuts)', was a colloquial expression of assurance to provide a government free of corruption. Modi's twelve-year regime in Gujarat proved to be the testimony to all his high-sounding pronouncements that people found convincing.

Given the diversity of the Indian electorate, strategizing for elections is more complex than playing chess in three dimensions. Having aligned his image with the mood of the nation and adequately backed it up by a consolidated rank of cadres drawn from the RSS, its affiliates and the BJP, Modi was acutely conscious of the fact that politics is not the sole factor that affects social life in India. There are many other factors, like spiritualism, religion, region, caste, traditions and culture, that play substantially significant roles in society. Similarly, he was also aware of the layers of political consciousness that keep changing with economic strata. At a rally in Hyderabad, an entry point for southern India and a hub of technology, he borrowed Barack Obama's slogan, 'Yes we can', in English. A few months before, he had addressed the students of the prestigious Shri Ram College of Commerce (SRCC) in Delhi and had adapted himself to an altogether different language of management and commerce. He would switch over to chaste Bhojpuri in Bihar or eastern Uttar Pradesh. He would use his phenomenal ability to change his demeanour according to the requirements of the circumstances.

But there is one lesson he seemed to have internalized, about deep-seated religiosity in Indian society. In his youthful years of wandering in the Himalayas and all across the country in spiritual pursuit, Modi had understood it too well that Indian society is permeated by a sense of spiritualism and religiosity, which determine the metrics of people's lives. Hence, his choice of Varanasi as his Lok Sabha constituency—besides also contesting from Vadodara in Gujarat—was guided by his instinctive impulse to connect to the two most venerated totems of Indian social life: the Ganga River and Lord Shiva, whose eternal abode is Kashi, the central part of Varanasi where the Kashi Vishwanath temple is located. In Hindu mythology, Lord Shiva and the sacred Ganga evoke pious sentiments cutting across geographical regions of the country. Kashi and Ganga are as revered in the south as in north India.

In post-Independence India, conventional politics had come to shun Hindu religious symbols. Gandhi was the only leader who never hesitated to deploy religious language and symbolism as an effective mode of communication in his politics. India's first prime minister, Jawaharlal Nehru, had shown a deep distaste for using religious language or Hindu symbolism, either in his politics or his governance. Nehru's aversion to Hindu nationalism got pronounced by the assassination of Mahatma Gandhi by a man who was called a 'Hindu bigot' and owed allegiance to the Hindu Mahasabha. In his political life, Nehru consistently faced stiff opposition from the Hindu Mahasabha, which relied on a battery of sadhus and saints led by Prabhudutt Brahmachari to pose challenges to his politics. This legacy of Nehru was assiduously nurtured by the Congress in the subsequent years. It was seriously challenged only when Advani launched his Rath Yatra in 1990 to demand a Ram temple in Ayodhya and was taken aback by the overwhelming response of common people to religious idioms.

However, no political leaders realized the untapped potential of a variety of religious orders and *matths* that held sway over the masses, till Modi began associating with those varied religious seats and symbols across the country. He continued his strong association with these religious centres to connect himself with a large swath of the masses, who tend to quench their spiritual thirst, combined with material comforts, through these centres in the absence of any institutional protection by the modern state. He would not hesitate to visit the matths run by the followers of Sant Ravidas or other such centres, in order to identify himself with millions of ordinary followers in any part of the country. The choice of Varanasi followed that pattern.

The beginning of the campaign was not smooth for Modi. He faced resistance from within and without. The time-tested alliance with the JD(U) came unstuck, as Nitish Kumar believed that his opposition to Modi would endear him to Muslims and eventually make him the tallest leader in Bihar. In 2010, Nitish Kumar, in alliance with the BJP, had practically decimated Lalu Prasad Yadav's Rashtriya Janata Dal (RJD) and romped home with a three-fourth majority. After Modi's projection as the prime ministerial candidate, Nitish Kumar sacked all the BJP ministers and came out of the alliance. He emerged as one of the bitterest rivals of Modi. His refusal to team up with Modi was seen as a setback, since Bihar elects forty Lok Sabha members and is thus a numerically significant state.

On 27 October 2013, the BJP had planned a huge 'Hunkaar Rally' (*hunkaar* means a clarion call—for change in this case) at the sprawling Gandhi Maidan in the heart of Patna. Modi, along with Arun Jaitley and other BJP leaders, was to address the meeting which was expected to be attended by a crowd overflowing the venue. This show of strength was marred by a series of bomb blasts that started going off in the morning. The first blast, which took place around 9.30 a.m. at the Patna railway station, was followed by more at the Gandhi Maidan in the afternoon. (Six people were killed and at least eighty-nine were injured over the day.) The police seemed to be missing in action, while the crowd was unmanageable. Sitting in the media gallery, I had a lingering fear that there would be hundreds of deaths if a stampede was triggered. But the BJP leaders and cadres at the venue handled the crisis efficiently and with maturity.

Though the improvised explosive device (IED) blasts could be clearly heard, the organizers from the podium described those sounds as the bursting of firecrackers by enthusiastic supporters and requested them to restrain themselves from using firecrackers near the venue. This cleverly invented deception prevented rumour-mongering and prevented the crowd from panicking. But what was really amazing was the response of Modi, who learnt about the blasts after his arrival at the Patna airport. As the huge crowd milled around the ground, it was impossible for the police to comb the place for any IEDs there. Therefore, the administration suggested that Modi should avoid the rally to prevent a serious tragedy. Modi declined the suggestion outright and told the officers that he would delay it for an hour to enable them to take preventive measures and then would go to address the rally. The moment he came to the stage, people's enthusiasm reached fever pitch. In the midst of the blasts, all leaders remained calm while the police were almost absent.

Modi's speech stood out for making an appeal to the audience to shun communal acrimony and work for the alleviation of poverty and betterment of society. The speech, punctuated with anecdotes connecting Gujarat to Bihar, and about the contribution of Bihar in the freedom struggle, held out a note of optimism, which people were so eager to hear. At the same time, his fervent appeal to people to brace up for the fight against 'poverty, illiteracy, disease and not against Muslims' had a very sobering effect on the large gathering, which did not get restive despite the blasts. Investigations later revealed that seven IEDs had gone off, while ten more had been planted near the Gandhi Maidan but failed to detonate. Four people were convicted in 2021 for planting those IEDs, and they were identified as suspected members of the Indian Mujahideen (IM) and the Students Islamic Movement of India (SIMI). Their aim was not only to disrupt the rally but also to cause a stampede, which could have claimed many more lives. It could also have triggered communal violence. Luckily, the IEDs were of low intensity and some of them malfunctioned, causing little damage. At the end of the day, Modi got unreserved compliments for remaining cool and composed against heavy odds at the Gandhi Maidan. This demeanour clearly won people's confidence right at the beginning of the campaign. He later also reached out to the families of those who died in the blasts and also those who were injured.

The Gandhi Maidan event had a nationwide impact. Modi's image as trustworthy and fearless was substantially bolstered, while those who tried to see him through a communal prism could not find takers for their political thesis. Modi travelled across the country to campaign for his own candidature and turned the contest into a presidential form of election. 'Your every vote in favour of the BJP would go to me,' he used to say in his campaign in order to emphasize that even if there were some reservations about the local BJP candidate, his or her victory would be deemed as Modi's victory. The personality of the prime ministerial candidate is often an important factor in Indian elections. Nehru and Indira Gandhi won elections on account of a curious combination of their charisma and legacy. Rajiv Gandhi had ridden on a sympathy wave after the assassination of Indira Gandhi to win elections. Morarji Desai and V.P. Singh were the prime ministers who emerged in people's perception as politicians with impeccable credentials and could rid the country of tyranny (of Indira Gandhi, in Morarji Desai's case) and corruption (of Rajiv Gandhi, in V.P. Singh's case). But both had to rely on crutches for their political survival. P.V. Narasimha Rao and Manmohan Singh were rather accidental prime ministers, with no political base. Lal Bahadur Shastri, Chaudhary Charan Singh, H.D. Deve Gowda and I.K. Gujral became prime ministers by sheer fluke and a combination of circumstances. Vajpayee was endowed with an exceptional charm and a gift of oratory that endeared him to the masses. Yet he had to rely on a coalition to run his government, with many interruptions. Modi's case was entirely different. He neither had a rich political legacy, like Nehru or Indira Gandhi, nor was he in the Vajpayee mould.

In this context, the determined attempt to turn the Lok Sabha election into a presidential poll was a rather audacious political move. A travel across the length and breadth of the country would make it clear that the election campaign was intensely Modi-centric in each of the Lok Sabha constituencies. It turned out to be a master strategy as it subsumed all local contradictions within the party's organization. At the same time it motivated the strong cadre of the Sangh Parivar to back the common cause of ensuring victory for Modi. When the campaign was at its peak, there was no ambiguity left in the rank and file of the RSS-BJP combine. What gave an edge to this intense campaign was a sustained appeal to voters to give a clear mandate to Modi in order to avoid exigencies of running a coalition, which successively proved to be a serious handicap for stable governance.

The pitch for a clear mandate found resonance among people whose collective memory of nearly twenty-five years of the coalition era in the country was that of a phase of degenerative status-quoism in terms of governance. After the Rajiv Gandhi government (1984–89), India always had coalition governments up to 2014. The Janata Dal experiment gave two unstable governments (1989–91), led by V.P. Singh and Chandra Shekhar, after which Narasimha Rao's government (1991–96) did last its full term, yet it was marked by occasional bouts of instability, indecision and serious charges of corruption. For the first time in independent India, the prime minister was directly accused of being involved in corruption in the Lakhubhai Pathak case and the Harshad Mehta scam. The inherent instability of the coalition came to the fore when the Jharkhand Mukti Morcha (JMM), a subregional group of Jharkhand in the pre-bifurcation Bihar, threatened to withdraw support and vote against the government in the no-confidence motion against the Rao government. The JMM support was bought over by paying bribes to the MPs in a brazen manner by power brokers on behalf of the government. These spectacles shocked the nation.

In 1996, Vajpayee became the prime minister for thirteen days as the BJP emerged as the single largest party in the Lok Sabha but couldn't muster enough support from other parties. In effect, the Rao government was replaced by two successive unstable United Front governments (1996 –98), led by Deve Gowda and Gujral, both of whom performed merely as caricatures of prime minister. Similarly, the thirteen-month Vajpayee government (1998–99) was formed by a disparate coalition that consistently faced uncertainties, and it fell after J. Jayalalithaa pulled the rug from under its feet. The second Vajpayee government (1999–2004) was relatively stable, though it found itself vulnerable when it came to taking firm decisions on account of various pulls and pressures from the coalition partners. The two stints of Manmohan Singh (2004–14) conformed to the same script when it came to dealing with alliance partners. The running theme of the coalition era of twenty-five years invariably revolved around the blackmailing or arm-twisting of the Union governments by those who had propped it up. After this history, Modi's campaign theme of appealing to people to give a clear mandate found resounding resonance among voters.

As the countdown to the election began, Modi emerged as the knight in shining armour in people's perception. Incidentally, this image was not built on any charisma but on account of deductive experience people had had over the decades. And the stage was set for an unprecedented political mobilization in the history of electioneering. On 5 March 2014, the Election Commission of India announced ten-phase polls in all 543 Lok Sabha seats for the 16th Lok Sabha—from 7 April to 12 May. Then the formal campaign began in earnest. Modi had a head start as he had been campaigning right from 15 September of the previous year.

By the end of the campaign on 10 May, Modi had travelled around 3 lakh kilometres and addressed over 435 public rallies and nearly 1350 rallies through innovative 3D technology across the country. He visited twenty-five states and most of the union territories in what could be veritably termed as a whirlwind tour. In each state, he tried to give a vision statement specific to that region. The organizational machinery was working overtime to distil information from every region and formulate a coherent agenda that could strike a chord with the local voters. Once again, the strength of the organization in getting the right inputs and using them for the right political messaging was on display in Modi's engagements with people across the country. In addition to these heavy-duty programmes, he held nearly 4000 meetings, 'chai pe charcha' (discussion over tea), and hundreds of other social programmes not connected with electioneering in order to connect with people. By the end of the campaign, Modi had directly communicated with an estimated 5–6 crore people through conventional and novel channels.

After witnessing months of hectic campaigning by political leaders, everyone waited with bated breath on 16 May for the results. The BJP alone was well past the halfway mark and had won a clear mandate by winning 282 seats. With allies, its tally reached 336. The mandate was unambiguously in favour of Modi as the BJP's vote share climbed to an unprecedented 31.34 per cent for the first time—up from 18.80 per cent in 2009 and 22.16 per cent in 2004. Modi had contested from two constituencies, Varanasi and Vadodara, and won both the seats. He went to Vadodara first to address a public gathering and gave a speech outlining his future vision of governance. His visit mollified the voters of Vadodara, as Modi had decided in favour of Varanasi as his Lok Sabha seat, giving up Vadodara. He later visited Varanasi, too, to express his gratitude to voters and promised to usher in change in one of the oldest cities of the world—a city that is believed to be the centre of the universe in Hindu mythology.

On 26 May, Modi was sworn in as the prime minister amid fanfare that attracted international attention. His swearing-in ceremony in the majestic forecourt of Rashtrapati Bhavan was attended by top leaders of South Asia, including Pakistani prime minister Nawaz Sharif and Sri Lankan President Mahinda Rajapaksa. The invitation to both was frowned upon by a section of political leaders within the country. But SAARC was represented in its full strength at the ceremony, which took place on an unbearably hot summer evening. Yet those who attended the function looked quite content over what turned out to be an epochal transition of the government.

5

The Promise | The Delivery | The Encore

A Knock Here, a Knock There, but Brand Modi Only Gets Bigger

(2014–21)

The swearing-in ceremony was the immediate task at hand as Modi drove into Rashtrapati Bhavan on 20 May 2014 to stake his party's claim to form the government. It was a hectic day for him. He had been earlier elected as the leader of the BJP's parliamentary party, at its meeting in the central hall of Parliament. Later, the BJP's allies endorsed his status as the leader of the NDA. Having finished all necessary formalities, Modi carried an eminently significant request to President Pranab Mukherjee, besides staking a claim to form the government.

Having spent long years in the government and engaged diplomatically with heads of states/governments across the world as a foreign minister, Mukherjee was widely respected as a statesman. Modi requested him to invite the heads of all SAARC nations, to give a clear signal to immediate neighbours about the friendly intentions of the incoming government. India's relations with Pakistan, of course, were not quite cordial after a series of terrorist attacks, including the 26/11 attack on Mumbai in 2008. Allegations of Sri Lankan forces' genocidal attacks on Tamils in the northern region of the island nation had raised the hackles of Tamil leaders in India and substantially disoriented the relationship between the two countries. Modi was keen to give an unambiguous message of a new beginning with a clean slate.

Mukherjee found the idea appealing and gave his go-ahead. Modi, as the designated prime minister, called Home Secretary Anil Goswami and asked him if he could ensure a glitch-free swearing-in ceremony, should it be attended by the SAARC leaders. Goswami assured that the event was easily manageable, and subsequently the plan was put into action.

The forecourt of Rashtrapati Bhavan is not the best place to be during the Indian summer. The gravel-paved courtyard in front of the sandstone building usually bottles up the heat, making it difficult for people to stay in the open for long. However, hundreds of the who's who of this country, along with the full SAARC representation, attended the function, as Modi and his council of ministers took the oath of office. He became the first non-Congress prime minister in independent India to receive a clear mandate from people, even though he'd contested as part of an alliance. Nawaz Sharif's presence was particularly interesting, as it ran counter to Modi's rhetoric against Pakistan during the election campaign.

An intrinsic requirement of statecraft is to keep messages subtle. During his stint as the chief minister and before the election campaign, a dominant section of the English news media, including foreign press, weaved a narrative projecting Modi as a leader who would rather prefer 'revanchism to reconciliation' as a state policy. The invitation to the SAARC leaders at Modi's swearing-in ceremony was intended to neutralize that stereotype. At the same time, the impression that the BJP was guided by the old and bigoted approach towards Pakistan was also dispelled as Nawaz Sharif was given a warm welcome and offered an opportunity to work together with India and turn a new leaf in reshaping the future of South Asia.

This event is once again reckoned as evidence of Modi's remarkable organizational ability to adapt himself to a new situation and reorient his image that might beat odds with people's perceptions. What is particularly significant is also the flexibility of the organizational network to play along Modi's tune on issues of national importance. The goals of governance got seamlessly aligned with the party's organizational objectives, a feat that had appeared quite difficult during the previous NDA rule led by Vajpayee. In the past, discordant notes struck by groups within the Sangh Parivar, particularly the Swadeshi Jagaran Manch (SJM) and Bharatiya Mazdoor Sangh (BMS), against the Vajpayee government often got amplified into a cacophony of dissent.

The grand spectacle at the swearing-in was also accompanied by an astute move to consolidate the party's rank and file. BJP president Rajnath Singh was inducted into the council as home minister and was replaced by the party's general secretary and in-charge of Uttar Pradesh, Amit Shah. In his address at the BJP's parliamentary party, Modi unequivocally complimented Shah for pulling off the spectacular victory in Uttar Pradesh by winning seventy-three (with alliance) out of the eighty Lok Sabha seats in the country's most populous state. The message was quite clear. Shah's anointment as the BJP president was a determined signal to keep the party in closer alignment with the policies of the government. Once again, the Gujarat experience played a crucial role in determining the priorities of both the new government and the party organization. Shah had worked closely with Modi in Gujarat and was fully clued into the functioning of the government and the organization.

The perfect alignment between the party and the government was the sine qua non for the future growth of the BJP. In the past, the BJP's experience with mass mobilization had been different. Its biggest mass mobilization had happened when Advani launched his Rath Yatra in 1990 to Ayodhya, on the issue of the Ram temple. Yet that mobilization did not have inclusive features in it. On the other hand, it contained a religious colour that alienated some social sections either due to religious or political predilections. Modi's experiments were different in nature. At the national level, that model was unveiled for the first time when he launched a massive mobilization campaign to collect agricultural tools for the building of the Statue of Unity near the site of the Narmada dam in Gujarat in 2013. The project to build a giant statue of India's first home minister, Sardar Vallabhbhai Patel, taller than the Statue of Liberty in the United States, was more a profound political statement than a whimsical endeavour. Modi, though not at the national stage then, mobilized not only the party cadre but also an army of his sympathizers around the nation to collect agricultural implements that would be melted to build the 182-metre-tall statue. It was promised that the contribution of over 5 lakh villages would be noted in a time capsule to be placed at the site for future record.

The whole project was unique and can help us understand a significant lesson of mass mobilization in India. Though the Statue of Unity project was executed in a highly skilled and professional manner by international technical experts, Modi's mobilization campaign made each village of India a stakeholder in it. All those who donated their agricultural implements came to develop an emotional bond with the project. In this method of mobilization Modi has developed and refined over the decades of his public life, one can see a distinct pattern even in the alignment of the government's programmes with the party's organizational pursuits.

On the face of it, there seems nothing unusual in having the two arms—the government and the ruling party—on the same page, but in India that is often not the case. The previous governments led by the BJP or the party's governments in the states had a different experience. The tradition began with the Congress, where the party apparatus would emphasize its independence. The Communist Party of India, too, favours an independent politburo. Sometimes the two sides are not in sync on purpose. It is not unusual to find a group of leaders in the government and the ruling party acting as a kind of internal opposition. That is a tactic aimed at representing a different view within the same party and not letting the opposition capitalize on it. It would be safe to say that for national parties it is the norm to keep the organizational agenda separate from that of the ruling side, though regional parties headed by strong leaders do not follow this practice. Such an arrangement, it is argued, promotes internal democracy. Notwithstanding its advantages, what it invariably does is create a dichotomy and factionalism, slowing down the processes of governance. For Modi, as chief minister and then as prime minister, the priority has always been to keep the two sides together, working in unison to boost governance.

That the BJP would lay as much emphasis on party-building as on ruling the nation was evident in its national executive meet in 2014, after the victory. The political resolution passed at the event stated:

> There is a lesson for the organisation in these elections. The wave of a popular leader and sentiment gets converted into votes where the organisation is strong and the local leadership is established. That is why it is essential to strengthen the organisation in all the states of the country and that is our responsibility.*

Having received the kind of popular support and mandate that no party had achieved in three decades, the BJP was by default bound to get strengthened as political workers and social activists gravitated towards the new victor. But the party

---

* 'Political Resolution Passed in BJP National Council Meeting at Jawaharlal Nehru Stadium, New Delhi', BJP.org, 9 August 2014, https://www.bjp. org/political-resolution/political-resolution-passed-bjp-national-council-meeting-jawaharlal-nehru

actively sought them out at the ground level with a membership drive. In March 2015, party president Amit Shah orchestrated a campaign to enrol new primary members. The response was more enthusiastic than anticipated, as about 1 crore names were added to the ranks within a week. That month, the party announced it had 8.80 crore members on its register. It also celebrated the feat of having become the largest political organization in the world, overtaking the Communist Party of China. A similar membership drive would be launched after the 2019 victory too, adding some 7 crore members. Today, the BJP has upwards of 18 crore members. That is just over 13 per cent of the country's population. As the current party president, J.P. Nadda, puts it, the BJP has more workers than the population of any country except the eight most populous in the world.

The quality of the data is open to debate, but it does point towards a broad trend. Moreover, the numbers can be corroborated by considering the accompanying rise in the income and donations received by the party. In 2012–13, the party had a total income of Rs 324.16 crore, which rose to Rs 673.81 crore the next year, with elections round the corner. In 2014–15, the income was Rs 970.43 crore, while by 2019–20 the figure had touched Rs 3623.28 crore, going by the income tax returns and donations details submitted to the IT Department and the Election Commission, respectively, by the party, as compiled by the National Election Watch.

Historically, parties start with a strongly articulated ideological vision but soon dilute it, either to seek acceptance beyond the core group or due to the exigencies of exercising power. Many of the leading political parties in India have stuck to this pattern. The BJP, too, came to power in the 1990s but as part of a coalition, and it had to keep the most significant parts of its founding vision in the deep freezer so as to win more allies and put together numbers to win power. What is noticeable about the rise and rise of the BJP under Modi's leadership is that it has come along with not a dilution of ideology but only an accentuation of it, as we will see in detail later.

This more substantial party backing would then add ballast to the governance campaigns. Modi had also realized from his Gujarat experience that the government's welfare programmes would not be a fruitful exercise unless they were adequately promoted and permeated people's consciousness. Besides the government machinery, the party's organizational structure is an effective tool to make people aware of these programmes right at the beginning. In Gujarat, Modi frequently announced welfare programmes with grand events at village, block and district levels by mobilizing people's representatives to raise the awareness level among the masses. Such party programmes in alignment with government schemes are effective not only in connecting the party cadre to the masses but also prove to be an effective instrument to gauge people's mood.

Governance divorced of a robust party organizational structure is a sure recipe for disaster. In his long political career, Modi had internalized this wisdom. At the national level, he tried to inculcate this spirit of perfect alignment between the government and the party. Now the question arose as to how one would devise welfare schemes that could be used as instruments of mass mobilization. People found the answer when Modi announced the Swachh Bharat Abhiyan, or Clean India Mission. The announcement was made on 2 October, the birth anniversary of Mahatma Gandhi, and the plan was in consonance with the vision of the Father of the Nation. Building toilets in all villages and making the country open-defecation free (ODF) seemed a tall order, but the mission has made rapid progress over the years. The essential feature of such a big enterprise was close coordination between the government and people. The building of toilets at a furious pace across the country was no doubt the biggest awareness drive for sanitation launched in post-Independence India. The BJP's organizational strength was deployed in full force to make this programme a success. For the party's cadre, it also offered the scope of getting educated in mass politics and profiting from it in the future.

Modi's articulation of women's plight due to non-availability of toilet facilities in significant parts of rural and even urban India struck an emotional chord with a large section of society subjected to this persistent ordeal. The massive mobilization drive of the government machinery in alignment with the party's organizational network created a favourable ecosystem for the BJP to grow in conjunction with the government. All these programmes were intended to expand the social influence of the party and made governance an effective tool for delivering measures for people's welfare.

Another initiative in the first year was the Pradhan Mantri Jan Dhan Yojana, aimed at making banking inclusive, taking banking services to every citizen, and thus bringing the socially and economically marginalized into the mainstream political economy. Such steps, though urgent and salubrious, were inconceivable in the past on account of the lack of political initiative. Within two years, nearly 26 crore people got connected to the banking sector with new accounts. Once again, a massive mobilization of the masses took place for a government scheme that was not at all connected to politics but aimed at welfare measures.

The content of Modi's programmes is markedly different from previous initiatives aimed at, say, poverty alleviation. For instance, Indira Gandhi's *'garibi hatao'* (remove poverty) slogan became popular in the '70s as the country was still grappling with food shortages. Privation was so pervasive that the rhetoric of poverty removal was enough to move the masses in Indira Gandhi's favour. As food sufficiency increased, her slogan changed to '*roti, kapda aur makaan*' (food, clothing and shelter) as the central theme of the political discourse in the '80s, the period that still laid emphasis on sustenance. Modi has effectively changed the discourse beyond sustenance and egged on people to ask for more. In all his programmes, his emphasis has always been on nudging the beneficiaries to overcome privation through government-assisted schemes. In his speeches, he would often decry those who glamourize poverty, which is supposedly preordained. Modi's poverty-alleviation programmes, right since his days as chief minister, were uniquely focused on giving a spur to people's ambition to climb the social ladder.

Perhaps there is no parallel to Modi's profound understanding of social psychology in contemporary Indian politics. He carefully devises government schemes in a manner that is connected with people's welfare at large without having overt political implications. Such schemes not only lend credence to the government's sincerity but also prove to be effective instruments to inspire the cadre.

The best case study of how well he comprehends the Indian psyche was his most audacious move, which in the hands of a lesser leader might have brought the curtains down on his career. On the evening of 8 November 2016, Modi announced the banning of currency notes of Rs 500 and Rs 1000 as legal tenders. Announcing this highly unusual move in his address to the nation, he delineated his objectives, which apparently were to check the accumulation of black money and terrorism funding in the form of counterfeit currency sponsored by the Inter-Services Intelligence (ISI) agency of Pakistan. He urged people to bear a little discomfort in order to have a better future. Conscious of the fact that such a move would inevitably entail suffering for the masses, Modi went ahead with this idea solely on the basis of his perception that the people of the country would not mind the inconvenience for a while if the intentions were good. Despite determined attempts by the opposition to whip up emotions on the issue, demonetization could not be turned into an effective rallying point for any protests. Instead, it proved to be politically beneficial for the BJP in the Uttar Pradesh assembly election a few months later, as the party won an overwhelming majority and nearly decimated the main opposition parties, the Samajwadi Party (SP) and the Bahujan Samaj Party (BSP).

Demonetization was indeed an audacious decision, as nearly 86 per cent of the currency notes in circulation were declared invalid within four hours. There had been a similar move in the past, when yet another Gujarati prime minister, Morarji Desai, had decided, on 16 January 1978, to declare the currency notes of Rs 1000, Rs 5000 and Rs 10,000 as invalid in order to curb black money. Those denominations, however, were of quite high value back then, and the move had hardly any impact on the general public. On the other hand, the latest demonetization had widespread fallout affecting all sections of society. People queued up to deposit old currency notes and withdraw new cash. In some cases, there were tragic reports of old or infirm people dying while waiting to withdraw their money. No doubt, such moments were politically delicate for Modi.

Yet, the way Modi came out of this phase can once again be attributed to his skills as an organizer and communicator. He consistently maintained communication directly with the people, following up his televised addresses to the nation with the radio programme *Mann Ki Baat* and emphasized that the travails caused by demonetization would be a temporary pain to relieve the nation of the malaise of black money and terror funding. At the same time, he deployed the party's massive organizational network in tandem with the government machinery to alleviate people's hardships. Party cadres fanned out even in villages to attend to the grievances of ordinary people. Soon, the discourse that emerged clubbed those criticizing demonetization in league with the corrupt, polarizing the debate in the binary of for or against black money.

Bihar chief minister Nitish Kumar, now on the rival side and in an alliance with Lalu Prasad Yadav's Rashtriya Janata Dal (RJD)—more on that later—quickly grasped the underlying significance of the move and lent his support to it. In his view, demonetization was more of a political project than an economic move. This assessment came true in the Uttar Pradesh election of February–March 2017, in which Chief Minister Akhilesh Yadav of the SP was battling for a second term, while Mayawati's BSP was the second-most powerful party in the legislative assembly. The BJP figured poorly at number four, even behind the Congress, after the 2012 assembly election. Though the BJP (with allies) had won seventy-three of the eighty Lok Sabha seats from Uttar Pradesh in the 2014 election, it was a big question if it would be able to replicate that performance in the state polls. Also heading for polls at around the same time were the states of Uttarakhand, Punjab and Manipur, though Uttar Pradesh was the most critical on account of its size, as the most populous state, as well as its importance, as the political barometer of the country.

Demonetization brought to the fore the issue of corruption in the Uttar Pradesh election. There was a time when the state was notorious for the brazen methods of fund collection by regional satraps. Though the veracity of stories then doing the rounds cannot be vouched for, there was a general impression that the past regimes of the BSP as well as the SP were mired deep in corruption. Demonetization was seen by people as an effective antidote to the prevalent parallel economy as the ill-gotten cash of the regional parties became invalid after the banning of high-value currency notes. In the face of public cynicism regarding corruption and the criminalization of politics, the BJP assiduously crafted a new narrative based on demonetization and promised to rid the state of criminals. Adding the epithet of 'anti-corruption crusader' to Modi's pre-existing image as a pro-development leader, the BJP's narrative overwhelmingly eclipsed the issue that would dominate every election in the state—of caste mobilization.

What appears to have made the BJP's task easier was a series of communal clashes that took place in parts of the state towards the end of Akhilesh Yadav's term. Rioting in Muzaffarnagar, Meerut and Hapur in western UP were serious in nature, while hundreds of small skirmishes along communal lines took place in other parts of the state. The emergent communal polarization also papered over the caste fault lines. Ironically, the SP was banking more than the BJP on this polarization as Akhilesh was keen to win over the Muslim votes lock, stock and barrel. The BJP, on the other hand, had carefully crafted its strategy of mobilizing its massive organizational structure and co-opting caste groups which were numerically strong yet politically marginalized in the state.

It would be instructive to understand the political trajectory of Uttar Pradesh to know how the BJP combined its organizational machinery, in tandem with the RSS and its affiliates, with the personal charm of Modi to make a successful electoral strategy. Before the polls, there was scepticism about the BJP's success, given the party's defeat in Bihar in 2015, in the face of a formidable combination of two regional parties—the JD(U), led by Nitish Kumar, and the RJD, led by Lalu Prasad Yadav. In the Delhi election, too, the BJP was thoroughly outsmarted by the Aam Aadmi Party, winning only three assembly seats in the seventy-member house immediately after the Lok Sabha election. Hence the BJP's invincibility quotient was substantially diluted in 2017, when Uttar Pradesh was going to polls. Since 1991, the BJP had never won a clear majority in the state, though it had won fifty-two and fifty-seven Lok Sabha seats in 1996 and 1998 respectively (out of eighty-five seats, as Uttarakhand was then a part of the state). Yet the party's performance in the Lok Sabha election had no correlation with its performance in the state elections. Why would 2017 be any different?

The only factor that was different this time was the presence of Modi as the Lok Sabha representative from Varanasi—in effect, as a leader from Uttar Pradesh. As the campaign built up, Akhilesh Yadav's SP was confined to its core base of the Yadav–Muslim combination, while the support base of Mayawati's BSP had shrunk to the Jatav community only. The BJP's support base effectively expanded to include the non-Yadav OBCs and non-Jatav scheduled castes, besides retaining its traditional upper-caste supporters. This was the biggest social outreach of the BJP, which had remained confined to the upper caste and some sections of the OBCs even in 1991, when it won a clear majority in the assembly under the leadership of Kalyan Singh.

When the election results came it stunned even the most optimistic BJP supporters. The party (along with allies) had made a clean sweep by pocketing 325 of the 403 assembly seats. It won 39.67 per cent of the total votes polled—an incredible feat in this state. The dominance of the BJP in the state's political space came to be almost monopolistic. The perfect blend of Modi's undiminished charm and the creation of a formidable organizational structure within the state was attributed as the reason for the landslide victory. Given the clearly unconventional mandate, the BJP leadership decided to go for an unconventional choice for chief minister. Yogi Adityanath, a mahant, or temporal head, of the Gorakhnath Peeth of the Nath Sampradaya, a Hindu ascetic order, was picked to lead the state. The selection was frowned upon by a section of the intelligentsia and opposition leaders, who held fast to the conventional notion of secularism. But all such objections were brushed aside as Yogi Adityanath was sworn in as chief minister on 19 March 2017.

Elsewhere, the party easily rode to power, as in Uttarakhand and Manipur, with the same political discourse, though in Punjab it was defeated by the Congress. The UP polls of 2017 were going to be the most important political battle between the two Lok Sabha elections of 2014 and 2019, and the BJP, led by Modi, had won hands down. During these five years, with Amit Shah at the helm of the party affairs, the BJP, for the first time, expanded its footprint into new geographies. Where it did not have sufficient workers on the ground, it managed to win over the ignored second-rung leaders from rival camps. Thus, the BJP came to power for the first time in Assam, Tripura and even in Jammu and Kashmir (though through a tie-up with the People's Democratic Party).

Yet, some states were proving to be the Achilles' heel for the party. Odisha was one. More interesting was the case of Bihar, always a slippery ground for the BJP for a host of reasons. In the state's traditional political culture, the socialist forces, with the peripheral existence of Marxists, occupied the opposition space, with the Congress playing the role of the principal pole. The BJP, or its progenitor, the BJS, always played a marginal role there. With the advent of Lalu Prasad Yadav in the post-Mandal phase, the political consolidation along caste lines, particularly in favour of the OBCs, became intense. This helped Yadav, who deftly developed his image of a secular OBC leader with pro-Muslim leanings. His credentials were further burnished by his decision as chief minister to halt Advani's Rath Yatra in 1990 and have him arrested. His theatrics, combined with calibrated rhetoric, helped him gain an iconic status as a secular leader of social underdogs.

In 1995, when George Fernandes, along with Nitish Kumar, parted company with Yadav, there appeared the first ray of hope for an alternative to the Lalu brand of politics. But his overweening dominance on Bihar continued till 2005. In the meantime, Fernandes and Nitish Kumar forged an alliance with the BJP in Bihar in the 1998 and 1999 Lok Sabha elections and the 2000 assembly election. Lalu Prasad got embroiled in the fodder scam and installed his wife, Rabri Devi, as the chief minister, and that gradually atrophied his political muscle. In the 2000 state election, Nitish Kumar was sworn in as the chief minister, but he had to resign soon as he could not muster up a majority. Rabri Devi returned to power and continued till 2005. The election held then failed to throw up a clear winner, and in the next election Nitish Kumar's JD(U), as part of the NDA including the BJP, was victorious.

While Nitish Kumar emerged as the undisputed leader of the NDA in Bihar, his relationship with Modi was going through many twists and turns, each impacting national politics. In private space, the two leaders enjoyed a very good rapport, yet they appeared at loggerheads in the public space. It would not be wrong to say that Nitish Kumar crafted his image as antagonistic to Modi in order to win over the Muslims in the state. He was desperate to wrest the support base of Muslims from his arch-rival Lalu Prasad Yadav's RJD, and he found Modi-bashing a convenient ploy to establish his pro-Muslim credentials within the NDA fold.

This was why Nitish Kumar persuaded the BJP leadership to keep Modi away from the election campaign in Bihar in

2005 and 2010, even though Modi, as Gujarat chief minister, was a star campaigner for the BJP across the nation. Since the 2010 Bihar assembly election saw the NDA, led by Nitish Kumar, winning nearly a four-fifth majority, it indeed spurred his aspiration for a national role. His rhetoric against Modi reached fever pitch and eventually led to his breaking away from the NDA when Modi was named the prime ministerial candidate in 2013. In the Lok Sabha election, Nitish Kumar's JD(U) was practically decimated in Bihar in the face of the Modi wave. The party won only two of the forty seats. Owning up responsibility, Nitish Kumar resigned and named his party colleague Jitan Ram Manjhi as chief minister.

Among the shrewdest politicians of our time, Nitish Kumar realized his political mistake and could foresee the prospect of his own marginalization if he were to go it alone in Bihar politics. Though Lalu Prasad Yadav's RJD was reduced to being a fringe player, the Yadavs and Muslims still supported it. Nitish Kumar forged an alliance with Yadav in order to consolidate his OBC support base and stem the tide of the Modi wave. In the 2015 assembly election, he was successful in staving off the BJP and formed a coalition government with the RJD. But the coalition was fragile, full of contradictions, and the domineering members of the Yadav family were keen to pull it asunder. Nitish Kumar was obviously not comfortable in the new company. Meanwhile, a prominent ally reached out to BJP leaders to bail himself out of a case of financial irregularity. This message was passed on to Nitish Kumar, whose discomfiture was growing every day.

What made the situation worse for Nitish Kumar was the release of the dreaded don and four-time Lok Sabha MP from Siwan, Mohammad Shahabuddin, from the Bhagalpur jail in September 2016. In a convoy of nearly 300 cars, he drove through the state in a brazen display of arrogance. Cocking a snook at the Nitish Kumar government, he declared his overt loyalty to Lalu Prasad Yadav while dismissing the chief minister as inconsequential. That Nitish Kumar had been drifting away from his coalition partner became evident subsequently. His position became further untenable when the CBI raided the residences of Lalu Prasad Yadav and his son Tejashwi Yadav, who was deputy chief minister, for their alleged involvement in shady land deals in Patna and Ranchi.

What is particularly noteworthy is the adaptability and readiness of Modi to turn the new political situation to his advantage. Having realized that Nitish Kumar still commanded respect among the electorate, Modi persuaded the BJP to keep a close watch on the situation and forge an alliance with the JD (U) if its Mahagathbandhan with the RJD broke up. Nitish Kumar finally decided to part ways with the RJD and submitted his resignation as chief minister on 26 July 2017. Within three hours, Modi directed the party leadership to work out an alliance with Nitish Kumar and run the coalition government. Sushil Kumar Modi, the BJP's top leader in Bihar, along with party MLAs, drove to the CM's residence and extended their support to him. The next morning Nitish Kumar was again sworn in as chief minister, with Sushil Kumar Modi as his deputy.

In a span of fourteen hours, the BJP had wrested an important state. The overnight political coup came about because of the growing internal contradiction within the JD (U)–RJD alliance. Modi, for his part, never stood on prestige and did not let the past acrimony with Nitish Kumar cloud his political judgement. As a result, in the 2019 Lok Sabha election, the BJP–JD(U) alliance won thirty-nine out of the forty seats in the state.

By then, of course, the five years in power had set the tone across the nation for the battle royale. The Lok Sabha election of 2019 was the first time the BJP was heading to the polls bereft of the shadow of stalwarts like Advani and Murli Manohar Joshi. Modi, his young team of ministers and young party leaders groomed by Amit Shah were in the forefront now. The five-year regime had created propitious ground in all corners of the country for the robust growth of the party's organization. State-level victories had boosted membership drives locally. The limitations that had handicapped the BJP's growth in the east, the North-east and the south were substantially overcome by roping in new leaders and expanding the social base. This strategy with the enhanced popularity of Modi had already put the BJP in the lead position, a place occupied by the Congress from Independence till the '90s.

In the first five years there appeared to be no ideological dissonance between the Modi government and the RSS. Unlike the Vajpayee regime, when the RSS and its affiliates used to take potshots at the government for deviating from the ideological standpoint, Modi's ability to check any drift was remarkable. Perhaps the one dominant reason for no bickering was Modi's personality, encompassing everything associated with strong nationalism.

This image was further bolstered when terrorists struck at a CRPF convoy in Pulwama, Kashmir, on 14 February 2019, killing forty jawans, just when the Lok Sabha election was around the corner. Once again, the opposition made the cardinal mistake of attacking the government, trying to expose the chinks in its armour. But that turned out to be counterproductive as Modi's promise of retribution against terrorists in Pakistan found resounding resonance among people. The subsequent Balakot air strikes, targeting a terrorist hideout deep inside Pakistan, reaffirmed Modi's masculine image as regards national security.

The subtext of strong nationalism was set ahead of the 2019 Lok Sabha election, in which the opposition leaders not only floundered but also scored an own goal by attacking the BJP in general and Modi in particular on national security. Modi was on the strongest wicket on this emotive issue while his welfare schemes earned him unstinted support of socially and economically marginalized sections of society.

For the seven-phase polling held between 11 April and 19 May, the suspense was not over who would win but whether the winner would be able to add to the tally. The results announced on 23 May did surprise many as the BJP was able to scale the 300 mark—something nobody had dreamt of. Modi was now in the select league of prime ministers who had won a second term on top of a full term—and he was the first from outside the Congress. Unlike the 'wave' of five years earlier, this performance was not based on expectations but on performance. What was common with the previous occasion was the winning formula: the presidential-style campaign based on Modi's image coupled with organizational reach-out at the booth level.

Though the record remains mixed at the state level, especially in places where the party has not had ground presence for long, it would not be an exaggeration to say that the BJP, under the Modi–Shah duo, has perfected the art of micromanaging elections. At the national level and in its bastions, it has become a veritable election-winning machine.

In the new term, Shah, who had been the BJP president since 2014 and got re-elected in 2016, shifted from the party headquarters to the government as home minister. Nadda, a minister in the previous term, took his place as the unanimous choice.

With this renewed and conclusive mandate, Modi had all the reasons to push for the ideological agenda—rather, he would be duty-bound to do so since the majority of voters had voted for his vision. By the halfway mark, the second term had been characterized by the Hindutva ideology in a far more pronounced way than in the first term, not to mention the previous BJP-led governments of Vajpayee. In particular, four long-standing demands had been ticked off the to-do list in quick succession, leaving actually little pending in the making of a 'new India'.

Within a couple of months of the new government's formation, in July, the government made the first move. The practice of 'instant triple talaq' in the Muslim community had been deemed unconstitutional by the Supreme Court in 2017. That year, the Modi government had brought a bill to end it, but it could not be passed for lack of numbers in the upper house of Parliament. On 30 July, however, the government pushed the bill ahead and got it passed too, amid walkouts. The move was debatable: on the one hand, the matter was something intrinsic to Muslim religious belief and hence part of the community's separate personal laws; on the other hand, it was clearly a medieval practice, committing grave injustice to Muslim women, and a liberal position would have favoured an end to it long ago. While the BJP supporters saw it as throwing in the dustbin a token of an exclusive Muslim identity, women from (and also outside) the community welcomed it as a measure of gender justice. Commentators saw it as a first step in the direction of a uniform civil code— one of those demands that had formed the very basis of the founding of the party's precursor.

The next move came within a week. On 5 August, Home Minister Shah tabled a resolution in Parliament to revoke Article 370 of the Constitution and thus the special status to the state of Jammu and Kashmir. Observers were too stunned to react to the move, so swiftly was a complicated conundrum consigned to history. Passed by a majority in Parliament, the resolution was thoroughly in order and there was little left for debate. The government went a step ahead and reorganized the state into two union territories—separating the Ladakh region. Jubilant BJP cadres burst firecrackers and distributed sweets in towns and cities across the country. For the votaries of muscular nationalism, especially the RSS, this historic step was making a decades-old dream come true. Placing the restive state under the lieutenant governor's rule before reintroducing democracy in a phased manner was also an answer to Pakistan-backed terrorism in Kashmir and elsewhere—the decisive answer the nation had been waiting for since the early 1990s.

By the end of the calendar year came the third move. On 12 December, Parliament passed an amendment to the Citizenship Act, granting legal status to migrants from Afghanistan, Bangladesh and Pakistan who had entered India before 2014. The crucial parameter was that this relief was offered to Hindu, Sikh, Jain, Parsi, Buddhist and Christian migrants who had been forced to flee after religious persecution. As with triple talaq, there were two ways of looking at it. The only denomination excluded was Muslim—and the community, as well as the opposition, felt it was being singled out. However, Muslims were the only community who would have no reason to flee any of the three neighbouring countries fearing religious oppression. On the other hand, for the six religious communities named, it was actually a humanitarian move, paving the way for their early citizenship.

The amendment to the law, however, came with the home minister's announcement of creating a National Register of Citizens (NRC). Such a register would necessitate proving one's bona fides. In the absence of any documentation, it was feared that the Citizenship (Amendment) Act (CAA) would offer a shelter to the rest but not to Muslims. The two matters put together, CAA plus NRC, created anxiety in some minds, and within a week there were widespread protests, leading to communal violence in the national capital in February 2020. Though the two plans have been put on the backburner, the government sent out a clear signal to its core support base that it was not going to make excuses of any lack of majority this time in implementing the Hindutva agenda.

The fourth historic move came on the first anniversary of the revocation of Article 370. The groundbreaking ceremony for the construction of the Ram temple in Ayodhya, in the eyes of the faithful, was an epochal event. Crores of Hindus had an emotional moment when they watched on their TV screens Narendra Modi performing the rituals on the sacred ground. For him, life had come full circle—he had coordinated a part of Advani's Rath Yatra in 1990 to campaign for the temple that was now coming up. Earlier, at the site that was believed to be the birthplace of Lord Ram, there stood the Babri mosque, which a mob of volunteers had brought down in 1992. Many strident voices had demanded the construction of a temple there, without waiting for a go-ahead from courts, since this was a question of faith. Modi was not one of them, putting full faith in the judiciary to resolve the complicated dispute over the ownership of land. He moved ahead only after the Supreme Court gave its final verdict and green signal in November 2019.

If we add to this list the inauguration of the Kashi Viswanath corridor by Modi in Varanasi in December 2021, the faithful Hindu would have little left to ask for. In his constituency, opening the revamped temple complex, Modi performed puja and also took a dip in the Ganga, wearing a saffron robe and a rudraksh garland. The symbolism was conspicuous, and it made a statement about the place of religion in his scheme of things. To further join the dots, consider Modi's frequent visits to the Kedarnath temple, his monitoring of its reconstruction and the plan to link the Char Dham—the four pilgrimage sites in Uttarakhand—with double-lane highways.

The repeated refrain from Modi and his colleagues of the making of a new India has its contours well defined by now. Its delineation would also include a nation-first foreign policy and a sounder defence of the borders, especially against China's nefarious expansionist designs. Delivering on the ideological agenda is also significant for winning the dedication of the party cadres, which would in turn feed into consolidating the organizational framework.

The grand project, however, faced an obstacle, albeit temporary, in the form of the pandemic in 2020.

The initial response from the government—imposition of a lockdown across the country at the short notice of barely four hours—was much debated for its timing and scale but not for its intent. And nor for its results. In fact, the nation not only supported but welcomed such a drastic measure in a replay of demonetization. It was met with no political opposition, and within no time a fifth of humankind had willingly decided to shelter at home. This would not have been possible except under a popular and respected leadership. The grand effort was also matched at the state level without any scoring of political points. Some expressed the fear that chaos would ensue, but it proved untrue.

The machinery of governance, now well oiled, ensured that the life of the nation continued. Modi helped the nation see opportunity in the crisis, and he gave the call for an Atmanirbhar Bharat—a self-reliant India. The only setback was the mass migration of labourers from industrial hubs to their homes, but the government was quick to offer them a helping hand at the earliest.

India was going into a war against the virus with two handicaps. First, the country's high population density and cultural diversity. Second, its public health infrastructure, which had obvious shortcomings as expected in a developing country. Yet, the nation put up a brave face and found solutions— from medical supplies to the setting up of health-care centres overnight and the manufacture of indigenous vaccines. The largest lockdown in human history was followed by the largest vaccination exercise in January 2021.

The second wave of COVID-19, with the more virulent Delta variant of the coronavirus, however, took the authorities by surprise. From March to May 2021, the governments at the Centre and in the states appeared clueless, with the hospitals overcrowded, medical oxygen in short supply and the number of infections crossing 4 lakh in a single day, a world record then. Just as Modi was given credit for the successful fight in the first year of the pandemic, he was squarely criticized for what many thought were systemic failures. While many commentators hold the government responsible for 'callous neglect', some experts believe that no system, not even in a developed country, could have withstood the tsunami of infection that the Delta wave brought.

The situation improved soon (only to worsen with the Omicron wave towards the end of the year), but for Modi, the crisis management involved the same elements as before: clear communication directly with people, backed by a reaching out on the part of the party organization at the grassroots level. Though in international commentary he is often clubbed with right-wing nationalist leaders, Modi has arguably been alone among them to stick strictly to science while responding to COVID-19. If we can believe the worst of the crisis is behind us in 2022, he has emerged from the test with his credibility largely intact. That would not have been possible without an active, inspired and committed cadre of foot soldiers on the ground.

Conclusion

An Organizer Who Never Loses Sight of the Organization

When political choices around the world are undergoing a tectonic shift, India, the biggest democracy, after decades of political instability has finally completed a revolution as it returns to the system of one-party dominance. When the rise of the BJP under the leadership of Narendra Modi is seen in this larger context, it seems the strategies and challenges in party-building have not received as much attention as they should have. The commentary has focused on the ideology, personality, social–political changes and much else, but not on what was happening inside the party machinery itself. Its growth has been seen as something natural or a corollary to all the changes outside.

This is not surprising. Myron Weiner begins his classic *Party Building in a New Nation: The Indian National Congress* (1967) by expressing surprise that few scholars and officials 'have given attention to the problems of party building in new nations'. The reason, according to the American political scientist, is:

> It is often presumed that while bureaucracies, armies, and educational systems are created in a conscious, deliberative fashion, parties are the products of historical change, impersonal social forces, or personal ambitions. Scholars generally describe parties as the outgrowth of parliamentary institutions, the result of the establishment of the adult suffrage, the product of ideological movements, or the

consequences of forces of economic modernization – almost
never as the product of a deliberate human act.*

This book has so far attempted to chronicle various small and
big 'deliberate acts' of Modi in building the BJP up to what it
is today. Now, in this chapter, we step back to take a broader,
theoretical view.

Though a young democracy, India has provided a vibrant
ecosystem for the emergence of a wide variety of parties that
serve as a bridge between the people and the institutions of
democracy. Today, political parties in India show a bewildering
diversity in terms of vintage, ideology, reach, geography,
internal structure and, of course, party-building strategies.

The Indian National Congress, established in 1885, is the
oldest among them all, and it has set the template for others in
terms of not only ideology but also the party structure, party-
building mechanisms, and the formal divisions of power and
informal channels through which it operates. Originally an
annual meeting of a club of English-speaking urban elites,
the Congress metamorphosed itself into a great political
mass movement with its presence across the country. Under
the visionary leadership of Mahatma Gandhi, it was the
chief platform of the freedom struggle. After Independence,
Jawaharlal Nehru and Sardar Vallabhbhai Patel were successful
in consolidating the nationalist movement into a political party.

Moving with the times over the seven decades since
Independence, the grand old party of India has undergone
many splits and transformations, but its essential structure
and character have remained the same: it is a mass-based party
(as opposed to a cadre-based party), with a centrist-to-left-

---

* Myron Weiner, *Party Building in a New Nation: The Indian National Congress*,
  University of Chicago Press, 1967, p. 1.

leaning outlook. In the words of Weiner, the party 'does not mobilize; it aggregates. It does not seek to innovate; it seeks to adapt.'*

The Congress has nominally retained its nationwide presence, and in times of elections it depends less on its own workers and more on traditional supporters (individuals or specific community groups) at large. This amorphous character—of its ideology, its leadership, its support system—is reflective of, one can argue, the idea of India itself. However, what has been its strength has proved to be its weakness, as the idea of India is apparently undergoing a makeover too.

The oldest party provided the mould, which others copied, improvised upon or reacted against. The first communist party in the country, the Communist Party of India (CPI), for example, modelled itself on its counterparts abroad and also adopted their cadre-based strategies of augmenting mass support. Innumerable regional parties, however, fashioned themselves after the Congress while introducing their own political views and objectives.

This, at first glance, shows the emergence of a simple classification: a party with a strong ideological foundation is likely to depend more on cadres, for the sake of ideological purity. A party with only vaguely defined ideologies, if at all, and more attuned to a set of broad-based values would prefer to interact with the masses keeping only a relatively small bunch of core workers. Another way of putting it is that there are parties that aim for the transformation of the country, and there are parties that are concerned simply with winning elections.

When the Bharatiya Jan Sangh (BJS), the BJP's forerunner, was founded in 1951, with help and support from the RSS, right from the outset it adopted a sharply different party-

---

* Ibid., p. 15.

building strategy, one that foregrounded the ideology and the indoctrinated cadre, and hence an organization. This is a defining characteristic of India's most powerful party in a long while, but the matter has not received as much consideration as it deserves.

As Deendayal Upadhyaya, the party's highly influential ideologue and mentor after Syama Prasad Mukerjee's demise in 1953, noted, stressing the centrality of the party structure, 'The votes are there if we can go out and get them, but for that we need organization and more organization.'*

Christophe Jaffrelot writes in *The Hindu Nationalist Movement in India* (1996), 'RSS workers within the Jana Sangh felt that the new party should avoid the practice of winning elections by co-opting local notables. Their technique of party-building was essentially long term and relied on a network of disciplined and dedicated activists.' Jaffrelot defines this 'Sangathanist' model thus: 'The strategy which they employed was "Sangathanist" in the sense that it relied on an integrated team of organisers (known as sangathan mantris – organizing secretaries) and was designed to ensure that the party's support was a coherent constituency rather than an assemblage of individual followings belonging to particular notables.'†

'Sangathanmantri' or general secretary (organization), incidentally, is a post somewhat unique to the BJP among Indian parties, precisely because of the paramount significance it attaches to the organization. This conception of party structure, relatively new in the Indian context, 'gives precedence to building a solid network of activists, capable at one and the same time of implanting the party at the local level through

---

* Craig Baxter, *The Jana Sangh: A Biography of an Indian Political Party*, University of Pennsylvania Press, 1971, p. 325.
† Christophe Jaffrelot, *The Hindu Nationalist Movement in India*, Viking Penguin, 1996, p. 114.

social work and of propagating Hindu nationalist ideology, albeit at the cost, if necessary, of unpopularity,' writes Jaffrelot.*

The RSS strategy makes all the more sense in contrast to the comparable case of the Hindu Mahasabha, whose rise and fall is quite an instructive lesson. As party politics gained ground in the country, the Hindu Mahasabha was the first forum that openly espoused the cause of the Hindus and co-opted even leaders like Lala Lajpat Rai, Madan Mohan Malaviya, Rajendra Prasad, Purushottam Das Tandon and many other stalwarts of the time. However, the most charismatic leader who had served the longest term as the Hindu Mahasabha president was V.D. Savarkar, who propounded the concept of Hindutva.

Savarkar was extremely articulate and endowed with a charismatic personality. He held radical views on religion and nationhood. Unlike the RSS, which confined itself to cultural activities primarily to promote a renaissance among Hindus, the Hindu Mahasabha was overtly political. Yet, as a political formation, it emerged like a flash in the pan of Indian politics and in due time was relegated to the margins of history. The reasons are not far to seek. In a pioneering research, *Militant Hinduism in Indian Politics: A Study of the RSS* (1951), J.A. Curran, Jr, bracketed the Mahasabha with the RSS as a potential challenger to the Congress dominance. The author, however, clarified in the preface, 'The RSS is by far the best organized and most ably led anti-Congress movement.' Incidentally, this study came out when the BJS was yet to be born.

The techniques and philosophy employed by the RSS were radically different from those of the Mahasabha, even though there was congruence between their core ideologies. The RSS stayed away from politics and started building its organizational network across the country by holding 'shakhas', or morning

---

* Ibid., pp. 151–52.

drills, of volunteers. The avowed objective was to rejuvenate Hindu society by acquainting it with its glorious past. In the process, the RSS expanded its base among the younger generation who found the ideals of nation-building appealing.

But right since its inception, the RSS was quite conscious of employing the means of social expansion that were legally tenable. The Mahasabha and the RSS couldn't get along precisely for this reason. This is significant in the background of Mahatma Gandhi's assassination leading to a six-month ban on the RSS and the organization's subsequent realization that a party compliant to the RSS's ideology was essential to express and defend its viewpoint. In 1951, Syama Prasad Mukerjee, a former president of the Hindu Mahasabha, was roped in to lead the BJS along with the trained cadre of the RSS. Mukerjee was a charismatic leader in his own right and had served as Union minister of industry and supply in Prime Minister Jawaharlal Nehru's cabinet. Though he was part of the cabinet at the time of Gandhi's assassination, he did not face any criticism on account of his ideological proclivity. He fell out with Nehru on a host of issues, tendered his resignation and founded the BJS—with a small function at a girls' school in Delhi on 21 October 1951.

In its initial years, the BJS largely borrowed from the RSS's techniques of organizational expansion. Its cadre formed the base on which the political party's superstructure was built. Though Mukerjee originally belonged to the Mahasabha, whose overtly pro-Hindu leaning was self-evident, he was counted among moderates in his political outlook. Within the BJS too, he induced a moderation which accommodated viewpoints not in conformity with those of the hardliners.

Mukerjee outlined his vision of the new party in his presidential address in 1953, which makes his moderate credentials clear:

Our party is open to all citizens of India irrespective of caste, creed or community. It would be a fatal mistake to confine the membership of a political party in Free India to sections of the people based on caste, community or religion. Equality of rights of Indian citizens, irrespective of any consideration, forms the basis of the Constitution of India, as indeed it must be a primary characteristic of any democratic country. Pakistan's recent proposals for basing her constitution, including minority rights, on Islamic law and principles of communal separation flagrantly expose the reactionary character of that State . . .

. . . Our party, though ever prepared to extend its hand of equality to all citizens, does not feel ashamed to urge for the consolidation of Hindu society, nor does it suffer from an inferiority complex to acknowledge proudly that the great edifice of Indian culture and civilisation . . . has been built most of all by the labour, sacrifice and wisdom of Hindu sages, savants and patriots . . .*

Mukerjee was quite aware of the reality that a political party's clout is directly proportional to its acceptance by the masses in electoral politics. He, therefore, made a determined attempt to expand the party's base among people.

A pamphlet known as 'Programme for a New Political Party' (with a preface by Mukerjee), written by K.R. Malkani, editor of the RSS-affiliated periodical *Organiser*, notes, 'If democracy has to live, parties must exist. Otherwise democracy may degenerate first into a one-party and then into a one-man rule.' This was a clear allusion to the dominance of Nehru in the early '50s and '60s. Malkani goes on to define the character of the Jana Sangh as reconciliation between traditionalism

---

* Craig Baxter, *The Jana Sangh: A Biography of an Indian Political Party*, p. 325.

and modernism. In *The Jana Sangh: A Biography of an Indian Political Party*, Craig Baxter quotes from the pamphlet: 'The good government of Bharat depends directly and fully on the formation of a nationwide party which will be as much revivalist of the ancient values as it will be futurist in its targets.'*

On his part, Mukerjee, in his first address to the 500-odd delegates drawn from different parts of the country, clearly outlined the route that the new party under his leadership would take. He said, 'We have thrown our party open to all citizens of India irrespective of caste, creed and community.' His declaration was unambiguously secular in its approach towards politics. With the help of RSS volunteers, Mukerjee launched a massive campaign to build the party's organizational structure by roping in individuals and groups converging on the political ideology.

Along with the BJS and Hindu Mahasabha, there was one more political formation devoted to the Hindu identity. The Ram Rajya Parishad, led by Swami Karpatri-ji Maharaj, had laid out an exclusivist agenda and developed a clout in certain princely pockets of Madhya Pradesh and Rajasthan. The BJS had thus to contend with two competing political parties, the Mahasabha and Ram Rajya Parishad, on the ideological front as they were quite open about their Hindu agenda.

Another handicap that the BJS had been consistently facing was the absence of an economic vision. While the Congress had openly espoused an economic policy with the underpinning of socialism, the BJS was pushing a political course in conflict with socialism, particularly of the Congress and Marxist streams. The Swatantra Party was the only formation which advocated liberal economic policies and free market, and opposed the state's control on the economy. A section of the BJS leaders

---

* Ibid., p. 60.

found familiar ground in that position, yet they were hesitant to take up the cause overtly.

Mukerjee's untimely demise in 1953 came as a shock for the party, which was yet to find its moorings in the political space. Yet the organizational structure, held together by those deployed by the RSS for political work, not only sustained itself but continued to grow phenomenally. Despite a long spell of turbulence that beset the BJS, in the absence of any charismatic personality who could replace Mukerjee and connect with people, it expanded its base in the urban areas of the Hindi heartland.

His successor, Deendayal Upadhyaya, was acutely aware of what would be required (and what had to be avoided) to make Mukerjee's lofty vision a reality:

> As a matter of fact electoral success is only a means to achieve the realisation of our ideals. We do have to amass popular support, but only of those who can follow our ideals and become one with our organisation. We do not simply want popular support; it must be idealistic popular support.*

He candidly acknowledged the limitations of that strategy, and those limitations remained in force for long as the party failed to make a mark for more than two decades of its existence.

In the late '60s, as anti-Congressism acquired the scale of a serious political challenge to the grand old party, the BJS gradually edged out the hardliners, the Hindu Mahasabha and Ram Rajya Parishad, and even appropriated their support bases and tactically aligned with anti-Congress political formations.

---

* *Organiser*, 26 January 1955, quoted in Jaffrelot, *The Hindu Nationalist Movement in India*, 1996, p. 120.

This phase saw the emergence of leaders like Vajpayee and Balraj Madhok at the national level, and also regional leaders like Bhairon Singh Shekhawat in Rajasthan, and Virendra Kumar Saklecha and Kailash Joshi in Madhya Pradesh. But much of the growth was attributed to the tireless work of silent builders, like Sunder Singh Bhandari in Rajasthan and Kushabhau Thakre in Madhya Pradesh. Both worked behind the scenes but had earned tremendous respect within the party.

Interestingly, the RSS gave a subtle hint of cooperation with the BJS in the later part of the '60s, even though the organization's strong cadre was always deployed at the time of Lok Sabha or assembly elections to extend support. And there is little doubt that the BJS's substantial growth was due to these thousands of full-timers and pracharaks who selflessly devoted themselves to the building of the party, right in the spirit of nation-building. In sharp contrast to the surfeit of articulate leaders across the rival political spectrum, the list of big leaders in the BJS was short.

It would be instructive here to consider the example of the Swatantra Party, launched by the redoubtable and erudite C. Rajagopalachari, whose connect with the freedom struggle, Gandhi and Nehru was the stuff of legend. He had also served as the last governor general of India, chief minister of Madras and Union home minister. He allied with yet another maverick leader, Minoo Masani, to launch a right-leaning party to counter the centrist approach of the Congress. Within no time, Rajagopalachari attracted key disgruntled Congress leaders, K.M. Munshi and N.G. Ranga, and emerged as a powerful alternative voice in politics. But in the absence of any organizational structure, the Swatantra Party gradually withered away without leaving even a trace of its presence.

The BJS, on the other hand, continued to focus on organization-building and adapted itself to the changing times, learning from the past to make way for the future. In the process, the party successfully filled the ideological and political vacuum caused by the atrophying of political forces which were ideologically similar but couldn't survive due to internal vulnerabilities. On the other hand, the BJS had cultivated a democratic culture of debate and discussion before arriving at a decision on crucial issues.

The difference between the BJS and other parties is aptly summarized by Craig Baxter, who writes,

> The writer's experience in attending political meetings is that the Jana Sangh operates somewhere between the near anarchy of PSP [Praja Socialist Party] and the 'no amendments' accepted procedure which had been typical of the Congress. The fact that a young saffron-capped Jana Sanghi could stand on his feet and suggest changes in the manifesto or in a resolution and not be rebuffed by some bigwig of the party led to a greater acceptance of the finished resolution or manifesto by the rank and file. Thus factional and programmatic disputes rarely occurred in the Jana Sangh.*

This was the precise reason why the BJS remained untouched by the inner dissensions leading to factional feuds, which marred almost all other political formations, including the Congress, socialists and communists. The BJS, no doubt, gained substantially in the 1967 assembly election in terms of political experience by participating in coalition governments (called 'Samyukta Vidhayak Dal') in several states, including Uttar Pradesh, Bihar and Rajasthan, and was a major political force in the municipal council of Delhi.

---

* Craig Baxter, *The Jana Sangh: A Biography of an Indian Political Party*, p. 60.

Yet the BJS had still not acquired a significant footprint across the country. Its area of influence was largely confined to the Hindi heartland, and the eastern and southern parts of the country remained beyond its reach. The party's social outreach was also limited to urban sections and upper castes, though it drew large sections of cadres from rural areas and OBCs.

Apart from the singular focus on 'idealistic' popular support, there was also the popularity of the Congress under Nehru to contend with. The masses continued to support the party that was at the vanguard of the freedom movement. With the advent of Indira Gandhi, there was a massive overhaul of the Congress, in terms of its vision, leadership as well as in its ways of winning power. In the early 1970s, however, her misgovernance and rising inflation were making her unpopular. A students' revolt in Gujarat in 1974 against Indira Gandhi spread across India and metamorphosed into a widespread agitation. Veteran socialist–Gandhian Jayaprakash Narayan assumed the leadership of this movement. The BJS then found a unique opportunity to expand its influence by aligning itself with this campaign.

Indira Gandhi, in reaction, overplayed her hand and imposed the Emergency, giving the opposition parties the first chance to gain popular support. The resultant political scenario brought anti-Congress forces together under the banner of the Janata Party, into which the BJS merged itself. For the first time, the BJS gained experience in leading a mass movement across the country by aligning with ideologically disparate political forces.

The short-lived Janata Party experiment and its disintegration make up a long story. But the group owing allegiance to the BJS came out intact, without much attrition in its organizational network and membership. When on 6 April 1980, a new outfit, the Bharatiya Janata Party, came into existence with the help of the leaders of the now-extinct BJS, Modi was not only a keen observer of these developments but also a participant. He was an active RSS worker during the Emergency, when Indira Gandhi banned the organization. (He was active in the underground and overground campaigns against the undemocratic and authoritarian moves of the government.) He assessed at close quarters the ups and downs of politics, which were often driven by personal ambitions rather than national and social interests. In understanding the course of politics, he acutely sharpened his social understanding and significance of the organization in sustaining a political movement. He was aware of the fact that the dissonance and discord between the organization and the government had been taking its toll on the Congress, which was gradually reduced into a motley group of family retainers and rent-seekers led by the Nehru–Gandhi family scions.

In this setting, the BJP began its political journey on quite a moderate note, under the leadership of Vajpayee, with 'Gandhian socialism' as its guiding philosophy. The term 'socialism' was not palatable to a section of hardliners within the BJP, yet the formulation came to be accepted. However, the party was jolted, making its electoral debut in 1984 with its worst performance. In the Lok Sabha polls held in the wake of Indira Gandhi's assassination, the BJP won only two seats as all its leading lights, including Vajpayee, were defeated. That was the worst phase for the party and the cadres that formed the backbone of its organizational structure. Since 1984, however, the country has witnessed only the rise and rise of the BJP, and this trend rarely faltered.

Though the Hindu nationalist ideology remained its unique identity, the party sought to connect with the masses on a host of other issues too. The Hindutva view also started gaining traction among the masses, thanks to myopic and power-centric policies of the Rajiv Gandhi government, as exemplified by its 1986 reversal of the Supreme Court judgment in the Shah Bano case on the one hand, and the opening of the locks of the Babri Masjid in the same year on the other. Rajiv Gandhi's successor, V.P. Singh, also inadvertently helped the BJP's cause by implementing the Mandal Commission recommendations for reservations for OBCs in education and government jobs in 1990.

Also, the two party presidents after Atal Bihari Vajpayee (1980–86)—L.K. Advani (1986–91, 1993–98) and Murli Manohar Joshi (1991–93)—campaigned aggressively on Hindutva, prompted by the dramatic moves of the two prime ministers of the late 1980s. They carried out a series of agitations and yatras (in which, as we noted earlier, Narendra Modi was a key organizer). The chief among them was, of course, the Ram Janmabhoomi movement, seeking to build a Ram temple at the disputed site of the Babri Masjid in Ayodhya.

The resulting phenomenal success of the BJP in the 1989 and 1991 elections would not have been sustained, were it not for the backbone of the party structure created and maintained by the likes of Kushabhau Thakre, with complete faith in the 'Sangathanist' model. Yet, the party was also evolving, and the times were tumultuous; some of the party-building strategies seemed outdated, and some new strategies seemed worth trying out. Giving the election ticket to 'notables' was one of them, as the BJP courted film and television stars (especially those associated with the two widely popular TV serials based on the Ramayana and the Mahabharata).

The party, however, remained true to the core of the original vision of the BJS founders, even as it tinkered at the margins. If the Congress system was conceived by a Western-educated elite and the Communist system was largely imported from the USSR, the BJP was the sole contender for the claim of a wholly Indian, home-grown way of party-building.

That was the time when Modi shifted from the RSS to the BJP and, in close coordination with the top party leadership, he began shaping the organization in Gujarat through his innovative methods of expansion. It was against the background of these events of the 1980s that Modi began his work of building and expanding the organization, as we have seen in the preceding chapters. If he was innovating techniques, he also remained committed to the core values as a long-time RSS pracharak. Unlike traditionalists within the BJP, Modi has always been acutely conscious of the reasons that prove to be the undoing of political parties that fail to adapt to the changing times.

Till the '90s, the BJP's organizational expansion was seen as the party's outreach among people through its trained cadres. Modi singularly changed the definition of expansion by including infrastructure as a basic necessity for the growth of the party. In the early '90s, he used to tour Gujarat and insist on building offices and membership registers to facilitate quick connection with workers. He adopted the same model in every state where he served, and deployed information and communication technology to enrol new workers. Looking at the large pool of younger people from urban as well as rural parts of the country, he egged on party leaders to launch a drive to enlist them and assign them a larger purpose in life—to contribute to nation-building. All young members were regularly called to training sessions aimed at inculcating in them a sense of discipline and purpose.

Modi's innovations in the states where he held the charge laid a solid foundation for the future growth of the party and attracted attention. In his role as party builder, he did not remain ideologically rigid and was seldom guided by prejudices or political dogmas. His decision to align with Bansi Lal in Haryana, despite the latter's infamy during the Emergency, is a good example. He found the old guard of the party in Madhya

Pradesh and Himachal Pradesh expendable, as they were not only outdated but also not well versed with the political grammar of the younger generation. Though he faced criticism, he stayed the course against all odds and won the day eventually. In Haryana, he tried to cultivate women as a new constituency for the BJP by promoting unconventional choices when it came to electoral candidates, like war widows.

There is a consistency in the party-building approach that clearly does not follow the path of conventional wisdom. In describing a leader, Myron Weiner, in his book *Party Politics in India: The Development of a Multi-Party System* (1957), writes, 'The leader has three key functions. He is, first, the compromiser of factional disputes. Second, he is the source of prestige to the members of the party. And, third, he is an absolute source for the articulation of values held by the group, and he may, as Gandhi did, articulate a new set of values.'[*] Modi, it can be argued, has performed all three functions with dexterity without losing sight of building the party organization.

In his role as chief minister, he honed the skill of seamlessly aligning the organization with the government's social programmes. He remains consistent even as prime minister to focus on the growth of the BJP, which has become the world's biggest political party. Unlike the National Democratic Alliance (NDA) government led by Vajpayee, which faced dissonance from the Sangh Parivar's constituents like the Bharatiya Mazdoor Sangh and Swadeshi Jagran Manch, the NDA government led by Modi remains in perfect alignment with the Sangh Parivar. He fits into the role of a 'classical sangthanist' whose tactical moves would eventually benefit the ideology in the long run.

---

[*] Myron Weiner, *Party Politics in India: The Development of a Multi-Party System*, Princeton University Press, 1957, p. 242.

At this stage, Indian politics has almost returned to single-party dominance, with the BJP looming large like a colossus and Modi as an indomitable giant among today's leaders from all parties. This scenario was inconceivable to even the most perceptive political observers barely a decade ago. How this change came about has been discussed in the preceding chapters, whose underlying theme is that the present is built upon a consistent and perspicacious approach of the BJP leadership, which quickly adapted itself to changing times. As Modi's stature grew and he achieved exceptional popularity, he went beyond the prevailing political idioms and lexicons in his dialogue with the masses.

Modi's eloquence, though much praised and a key aspect of his image, was no match to Vajpayee's oratorical prowess. But for an impatient young India tired of old political platitudes, Modi's style, dramatic touches, punchlines and engaging tone found instant traction in the post-Vajpayee era. His attraction was as much visible in the south as in the Hindi heartland. Across the country, he managed to evoke hope among people who were looking for a political alternative. In the course of my interactions with him, Modi insisted that he does not believe charisma alone can sustain people's trust for long. There are a number of political personalities endowed with exceptional charm, yet it can do little for them. That is why Modi consistently refers to Mahatma Gandhi to contextualize his politics. He believes in taking his ideas to the masses and getting their acceptance as an index of approval.

Arguably, the secret of Modi's success in groundbreaking methodological innovations is remarkable flexibility. The underlying pragmatism of the RSS encourages and welcomes creative and radical departures from the playbook. Ever since his induction in the party, Modi has deployed unorthodox techniques, caring little for the old-fashioned dogmatic ways of expanding the organization. Yet, he met with no censure. Indeed, his ways were accommodated within the Sangh's scheme of things. This lack of rigidity and openness to experimentation comes naturally to the Sangh Parivar, which sees in this approach an Indian way of dealing with reality. Most outsiders miss this open secret.

That factor—flexibility—is the unacknowledged inherent reason for the BJP's growth. If the history of the Sangh Parivar is to be judged in the right context, it readily embraces the ideas that may not be ideologically compatible but get social traction. The Congress dominance, with the Nehru–Gandhi family at the top, is understood by Modi as a 'civilizational disruption' in the absence of personalities like Mahatma Gandhi. In 1967, 1975 and 1989, people expressed their deep desire for a change which was temporarily, rather cunningly, crushed by the Congress. Its imposition of President's rule on non-Congress state governments was indicative of its inability to come to terms with regional aspirations.

Modi seems to be making no such mistakes. That he would not stand on prestige despite his image of a strong leader was evident when he withdrew the three bills on agriculture reforms in late 2021. The moment he realized that the bills were being taken as a pretext to foment a subversive movement not only within India but also by external forces, he declared his intention to withdraw the legislative move 'in the larger interest of the nation'. He also apologized, underlining that his intent was benevolent but he might have erred in judgement. Modi perhaps stands alone in contemporary politics for having taken decisions that entailed hardships for people. Demonetization and the lockdown amid the pandemic are good examples. But he always owns up his responsibility for each of them and never indulges in passing the buck. None of those difficult decisions have caused any erosion in people's trust in Modi or in the credibility of his government, because people do not find any fault with his intentions.

Right since the beginning, Modi has kept on emphasizing three critical aspects of his working style to win the trust of the masses. First: 'I will leave no stone unturned for the benefit of the people and the nation.' Second: 'I will do nothing for personal gain.' Third: 'I may make bona fide mistakes but won't do anything with bad intentions.' These three messages from him seem to have hit home, not only with the ever-growing party cadre but also among the party's support base. As a result, the BJP has achieved a scale of dominance attained by the Congress immediately after Independence that continued for decades.

It would be patently naive to attribute the growth of the BJP to Modi's charisma alone. Far from it, the legacy bequeathed from the BJS to the BJP is such that it continues to emerge stronger, while a mass-based party like the Congress and a strong and ideologically motivated cadre-based party like the Communist Party of India (Marxist) have been relegated to the margins. In states where regional parties are stronger, the BJP leadership has consciously avoided coming in conflict with the regional sentiments, be it Punjab, Andhra Pradesh, Telangana, Tamil Nadu, West Bengal or Odisha. In Bihar, the party, though a majority partner in the alliance, conceded the chief ministership to its ally, Nitish Kumar.

There is no doubt that Modi is politically astute. He carefully crafts his strategy to win elections. But that is what every politician is supposed to do. The real story of Modi's success lies in his genius for organization building, which he had so assiduously learnt from a generation of leaders from the Sangh Parivar and applied it successfully over the decades.

At this point, the question arises as to what the BJP's future will be under Modi and beyond him. Perhaps a decade back, the prospect of a BJP government getting a resounding mandate looked a remote possibility. In the early '90s, such an idea was not even worth wasting your time on. Things changed in the past two decades, and the BJP achieved the dominant position in Indian politics. Will this dominance be transient or will it last long?

It will be interesting to analyse these pertinent questions in the context of the organizational growth of the BJS/BJP.

Right since its inception, the party might have appeared to be fixated on its specific ideological goals, but it had always shown openness to adapting to the exigencies of Indian politics. In its initial phase of growth, it clearly lacked experienced political leaders, except for Syama Prasad Mukerjee. After Mukerjee's demise, its leadership largely comprised those who were trained RSS volunteers. Hence, they lacked the nimble-footedness of those leaders who were adept at negotiating the labyrinth of Indian politics.

The party leadership initially fumbled but gradually adapted itself to the changing political circumstances. By the third parliamentary election, the BJS had acquired enough political muscle to pose a formidable challenge. Though the party leadership was never shy of its ideological moorings, inextricably rooted in the RSS, they were allowed complete autonomy to take political decisions for the growth of the party. When Deendayal Upadhyay joined Ram Manohar Lohia in endorsing a proposal to create a federation of India and Pakistan, it was clearly in conflict with the Sangh Parivar's initial concept of 'Akhand Bharat', or undivided India. But Upadhyay was allowed to take a pragmatic view of the situation.

The party's decision to join the JP movement in 1974 was not impulsive but driven by political pragmatism. Similarly, the BJP supported V.P. Singh in his anti-corruption movement against Rajiv Gandhi despite Singh's often unfriendly utterances. In the course of its political journey, the BJS/ BJP not only gained experience in mass movements but also expanded its organizational network to get real feedback from the ground. This helped the party leadership in getting a feel of the pulse of the people. It has developed a unique mechanism of feedback from the ground and specific directions for the cadre to carry out programmes.

When Modi started campaigning for the 2014 Lok Sabha election, cadres galvanized into action as they could see that he was gaining exceptional popularity. Modi, through his innovative methods (discussed in previous chapters), not only expanded the organization phenomenally but also made inroads into eastern and southern India by co-opting mass-based leaders into the party's fold. The party has consciously groomed a large number of next-gen leaders, at both national and regional levels, who have also been learning expansion methods from the top leadership.

As of now, the BJP has successfully filled the vacuum caused by the exit of the Congress as a national party. Unlike the Congress, which degraded its vast organizational network and rendered it effete, Modi ensures that the organization is not a political expedient for the government. He has created a unique harmony between the government and the organization, which never existed before. This predominant political position is unlikely to be unsettled in a post-Modi phase, as he will be leaving behind a robust political structure that will keep on creating its own icons of the time.

Acknowledgements

Writing a short news report comes quite easy to a reporter. Writing a book, however, requires a great deal of perseverance, research and collaboration at various levels. This book is my first attempt at writing a longer work, and it has been quite a humbling experience in more ways than one. Despite painstaking research and long hours of writing, you keep wondering if you are missing something, if you are drawing the right conclusions. Such questions are bound to crop up all the more when the book is an attempt to unravel a specific facet of a political leader like Prime Minister Narendra Modi. Much as I have tried to keep the focus on his party-building techniques, the topic appears to be very broad and without predefined boundaries.

The project was challenging, and it might not have been completed but for the help from so many quarters.

In the process of collecting facts, I interviewed hundreds of people, ranging from the party's national leaders to village-level workers, to ascertain the details of the party-building model. And each interview has given me insights into the fundamentals of Indian politics, especially how the making of a vibrant political organization is an essential and natural corollary to political success. I am grateful to all of them for sharing their experiences of Modi's organizational skills.

I express my gratitude also to others—leaders of domains other than politics who shared their views on the topic. I remain indebted to all news organizations I have worked for and many colleagues there—too many to name. Still, I would like to name some whose help was crucial in the writing of this book.

I first met Mahesh Rangarajan in 1993, when we were both working with the *Telegraph*. His eagerness to learn more about ground-level politics was perfectly complemented by his profound understanding of history. He later became an academic of international repute. I have invariably turned to Mahesh to learn more about the historic aspects of party-building in India. As usual, he has been generous in providing me with reading material and explaining the long-term perspective. He has been an extraordinary help in formulating my ideas about this book.

After long years in print media, when I switched to TV journalism, I was fortunate in having an inimitable boss and mentor, Uday Shankar, who has the rare skill of combining the roles of a hardcore journalist and a management guru. He would always keep the bar of excellence very high in order to motivate me. He has been a source of strength and inspiration.

I consider myself lucky in having a senior colleague like B.V. Rao, with whom I worked in three organizations—STAR News, *Governance Now* and Firstpost. An amiable editor, he always put immense faith in me and nudged me to undertake this book project.

When the research for this project required dedicated time and travel, I needed to take a break from the regular work of editing *Governance Now*, the fortnightly magazine we had launched in 2010. Markand Adhikari, its indulgent and resourceful promoter, made it possible for me to spare more time for this project.

If I find myself in doubt or despair, Rohit Bansal will not only act as a saviour but also come up with unconventional remedies. I have immensely profited from his wisdom when it came to taking this project to its logical end.

Ashish Mehta's support in giving shape to this project has been critical. Though younger in age, Mehta, a valued colleague and friend, contributed immensely in enriching the content with his profound and scholarly understanding of society and politics, particularly with reference to Gujarat.

I was appointed as press secretary to the President of India on 1 October 2019. Though I had completed my research before the beginning of my stint in the government, a portion of critical writing was yet to be completed. The beginning of 2020 saw the outbreak of the pandemic that almost paralysed the office routine. I used that period for further research and writing. In this assignment in the government, I have found excellent colleagues and seniors who were not only considerate but helpful in letting me complete this pursuit. I am grateful to all of them.

I must thank Milee Ashwarya, publisher at Penguin Random House India, and her team for guiding a first-time author through the process and making this book more reader-friendly.

This book has taken more than four years to complete. It has been a period punctuated by my switching of jobs and the outbreak of the pandemic. But I was fortunate to get adequate time from Prime Minister Narendra Modi to hear his views on party-building and also learn more about certain aspects of his political life. He was so forthcoming in these interactions that my momentary hesitation dissipated.

My wife, Dr Anjali Singh, is an associate professor, and carries that mantle at home as well. I don't know how many times she chided, goaded and cajoled me not to delay the project any further. She would add to my guilt complex in order to motivate me to wrap up what I had begun four years back. My daughters, Apurva and Shreya, were very enthusiastic to see the project through. My mother, Ram Singari Singh, who died of old age in 2020, knew I was writing a book on Prime Minister Modi. She was glad about the project as she adored him a lot. I dedicate this book in her memory.

Bibliography

Numerous documents of the Government of Gujarat and the Government of India, especially the budget papers, were consulted in the writing of this book. They are not included here. Also, no reference is made here of news reports (including the author's own ground reporting and analyses) relating to specific events. Certain key works that help in the understanding of the theoretical questions underpinning this book are as follows.

Walter K. Andersen and Shridhar D. Damle, *The Brotherhood in Saffron: The Rashtriya Swayamsevak Sangh and Hindu Revivalism*, Vistaar Publications, New Delhi, 1987.

Craig Baxter, *The Jana Sangh: A Biography of an Indian Political Party*, University of Pennsylvania Press, Philadelphia, 1971.

J.A. Curran, Jr, *Militant Hinduism in Indian Politics: A Study of the RSS*, Institute of Pacific Relations, New York, 1951.

Bruce Graham, *Hindu Nationalism and Indian Politics: The Origins and Development of the Bharatiya Jana Sangh*, Cambridge University Press, New York, 1990.

Zoya Hasan (ed.), *Parties and Party Politics in India*, Oxford University Press, New Delhi, 2004.

Christophe Jaffrelot, *The Hindu Nationalist Movement and Indian Politics: 1925 to the 1990s, Strategies of Identity-Building, Implantation and Mobilisation (With Special*

Reference to Central India), Viking Penguin, New Delhi, 1996.

Pralay Kanungo, *RSS's Tryst with Politics: From Hedgewar to Sudarshan*, Manohar, New Delhi, 2002.

Sanjeev Kelkar, *Lost Years of the RSS*, Sage Publications, New Delhi, 2011.

Utpal Sandesara and Tom Wooten, *No One Had a Tongue to Speak: The Untold Story of One of History's Deadliest Floods*, Prometheus Books, New York, 2011.

Myron Weiner, *Party Politics in India: The Development of a Multi-Party System*, Princeton University Press, Princeton, 1957.

Myron Weiner, *Party Building in a New Nation: The Indian National Congress*, University of Chicago Press, Chicago, 1967.